Little Sermons on Sin

LITTLE SERMONS ON

SIN

The Archpriest of Talavera

BY ALFONSO MARTINEZ DE TOLEDO

Translated by Lesley Byrd Simpson

UNIVERSITY OF CALIFORNIA PRESS
BERKELEY, LOS ANGELES, LONDON

University of California Press
Berkeley and Los Angeles, California

University of California Press, Ltd.
London, England

©1959 by the Regents of the University of California
Reissued 1977

ISBN 0-520-03281-0
Library of Congress Catalog Card Number: 59-5746

Designed by Adrian Wilson
Printed in the United States of America

⌐ Contents

PART TWO

PART THREE

Alfonso Martínez de Toledo, author and hero of the book that, I hope, you are about to read, was a pulpit-thumping, roaring, sneering, malicious, lusty, and, with it all, a sincere and immensely energetic denouncer of sin. He finished his book in 1438, at a time when morals were loose and the town life of Castile was uninhibited. His book is very likely the noisiest ever written, partly because the Archpriest loves the sound of his own voice, partly because he has to make himself heard above the squalling viragoes he is preaching at. He is obsessed with the incorrigible cussedness of mankind, or rather, of womankind. His clinical eye misses no weakness. He takes the utmost delight in digging up gruesome or comic illustrations of his theme, drawing on the stock in trade of mediaeval preachers: such hoary chestnuts as the story of Virgil hanging in his basket, Aristotle ridden by his mistress, Samson and Delilah, David and Bathsheba, and the like. But he depends much less upon book learning than upon the vastly richer treasure house of his own life. He has, indeed, a thinly veiled contempt for armchair moralists. Experience is the only teacher. He is a practical man.

"Reading about such things," he says, "is profitable, to be sure, and understanding them is a help, but practice and experience are the best teachers. . . . What one man went through, with many hardships and dangers and suffering, and what he saw in his own person and wrote down on a piece of paper, let this teach others and serve as a lesson against evil-doing, a remedy for wickedness, and a warning against the pitfalls of this world, and serve to protect and defend them from the devil and from women."

Women! Here the good Archpriest is on solid and chosen ground. He knows all about the exasperating creatures: the most intimate details of their wardrobe and dressing table, their infinite wiles, and the endless catalogue of their vices, which he recites with a mocking and infectious hilarity. The only time he permits a note of bitterness to intrude is when he denounces them for their outrageous treatment of the clergy. His types are drawn with a sure touch and extraordinary economy. He allows his women (and this is close to genius) to portray themselves. The avaricious woman, the envious woman, the gossip, the drunkard, the disobedient wife, and the rest, are brought to life in a series of shrill tirades, as graphic as they are comical, in the gamy language of the town square and the market place, punctuated and seasoned with good Castilian salt. Women are wicked, no doubt about it, although the Archpriest discovers some excuse for the young and beautiful, beset as they are by temptation on every hand, poor things. For the old and ugly, on the contrary, he has no sympathy whatever. He brings his heaviest guns to bear on the old woman "no longer of this world" who flaunts her faded beauty in the square, and on the ancient prostitute, now out of the running, who leagues herself with the devil and turns for a living to the casting of spells and love charms, in which, incidentally, the Archpriest firmly believes.

Men are clearly less exciting, but they come in for some tremendous thumps just the same. The proud lover, the amorous friar, the lively scholar, the undutiful son, the old husband of a young wife, and the various complexions of men are drawn with equal skill, freshness, and absence of tenderness.

It is this kind of impish reporting that convinces me that the Archpriest is shaking with laughter a good part of the time, even as he wags a monitory finger. This is not to doubt his sincerity. He is the reformed rake reliving his rakish past with many a nostalgic glance over his shoulder, beating his breast and sighing the while. His recital of the choleric man's misadventures has the ring of reminiscence. The choleric man gets himself into a pot of trouble on account of his mistress and has to fly the country. "He will lose his possessions and live in hiding and run away, abandoning his country and his house, and will wander about in foreign parts, making a living for magistrates, constables, and notaries, and all because of those accursed, damned, unlucky, poisonous, cruel, and monstrous tears! O Lord, would that I could weigh the tears of a woman, had I but the knowledge! Truly, a single tear of hers outweighs a hundredweight of lead or copper!"

The Archpriest's book is so crowded with such personal incident and observation that it is tempting to try to reconstruct his early life from them. We know little about him otherwise. According to his own statement on the title page, he was born in 1398. We know nothing of his family—which in itself is odd, because he must have been a fairly

eminent man to be appointed chaplain to the king.
He evidently enjoyed the protection of someone of
high position, for he was sent through college and
given a benefice in Toledo at the very tender age of
seventeen. There is some reason to suspect that he
was the natural son of one of the higher clergy. In
his bitter chapter on "How the priest and even the
layman are destroyed by love" we may have a clue
to his origin. "There is not a woman in the world,"
he says, "who does not hate ecclesiastics worse than
poison. . . . And from this rule I do not except the
laity, even though they are the sons of priests."
Earlier in the same paragraph he makes another re-
vealing remark: "I have never seen an ecclesiastic
. . . who has succumbed to dishonest love and won
benefices or honors in God's Church." In his chapter
on "How marriages are destroyed by love" we have
what looks like another bit of evidence. Speaking of
bastards he says: "Such a son is deprived of his
paternal heritage as a punishment for the accursed
coitus. Moreover, he is ineligible for all temporal
honors, and even the Church will never allow him to
hold a benefice unless he is first legitimized by the
pope, or by his bishop, who in this case may give
him permission to hold a benefice or two, but not
the ones he would choose for himself." *

---

*My friend Luis Monguió who, for my sins, is a Gradu-
ate in Law, stopped me at this point. "Hold on!" he said. "I
can't go with you there. That is not evidence of personal
experience. The Archpriest is merely repeating a commonplace of mediaeval law, which you will find in the *Siete
Partidas* of Alfonso the Wise, Ley II, Título XIII, of the
Cuarta Partida." And he clinched his argument with three
or four other citations of equal gravity, civil and canonical.
He did admit, however, that the last clause of the quotation
might be construed to support me. My defense was that it
could be a legal commonplace and a personal experience at

Whether or not such speculation is justified, it is a safe guess that at seventeen the lad was still untamed, for a little later we find him in Barcelona and the eastern provinces, perhaps in exile, where he spent eight years acquiring the rich stock of experience with which he illustrates his sermons. He may have changed his ways, for in 1427 he was back in Toledo, although his benefice was not restored until 1436, by a bull of Pope Eugene IV—which in itself is a strong indication of favor in high places. Two years later, as a kind of *mea culpa* and earnest of his reform, he finished *The Archpriest of Talavera*, written to save others from his own dreadful life of sin which, of course, he now deplores, although it was a lot of fun while it lasted. "And if anyone," he concludes, "reads what I have said here and puts it into practice, I pray God that his mending will serve to redeem a few of the sins I once committed, as well as those I commit each day, and, after I am dead, win me pardon for this life of pain and torment, amen!" The Archpriest is now an ancient of forty.

Martínez de Toledo lived most of his life during the long reign of the insignificant John II of Castile (1405–1454), who began his rule at the age of twenty-two months and was declared of age at fourteen years. John soon found the task of dominating his turbulent nobles too much for him and turned the power over to his favorite, the magnificent Don Alvaro de Luna, whom he ungratefully beheaded in 1453, just before yielding up his own pale spirit. It was the glorious time when the full tide of the Renaissance was sweeping over Spain. Art, architecture, letters, and learning became fashionable.

the same time, so I am leaving it at that and adding this note to clear my learned friend of any suspicion of complicity.

Great nobles, such as the Marqués de Santillana, the Marqués de Villena, and a host of others discovered that exquisite verse and prose were not necessarily at odds with manhood. The puritanical reforms of Isabella the Catholic and Cardinal Ximénez de Cisneros, with their grim engine of suppression, the Holy Office, were in the future. Uncensored and unchecked, the fifteenth century produced a flowering of letters unique in the history of Spain, with Italianate refinement at the top and Castilian bawdiness at the bottom. Whether he knew it or not, the Archpriest of Talavera supplied the salutary earthiness that kept Humanism humane, following in this the footsteps of his famous predecessor and fellow archpriest, Juan Ruiz. Our Archpriest's great contribution was his discovery of the limitless possibilities of the vernacular. His book became the treasure chest into which later writers dipped with both hands, notably the author of *The Celestina*, whose genius brought the two levels of the Renaissance together in one of the most original works of any literature.

So great is this debt that it is difficult to imagine *The Celestina*, at least in its living portrayal of low life, being written without the Archpriest to lean upon. Old Celestina herself, with her charms and spells and league with the devil, is prefigured in the Archpriest's witch. Her salty speech and penchant for clinching an argument with a proverb come straight from him. Her lively "daughters" repeat almost verbatim the diatribes of his envious woman. Celestina's reflections on the morals of the clergy are his. This is not to argue that the two books are comparable. *The Celestina* is an admirably constructed and consummate work of art; *The Archpriest of Talavera* is a collection of shrewd and intensely personal observations on the follies of mankind, loosely hung upon a moral framework. It is the prototype of the novel of roguery which has been with us ever since, and, as I said at the beginning, the Archpriest is his own hero.

The only surviving contemporary manuscript is that copied by the somnolent Alfonso de Contreras in 1466, and it is so full of obscurities, misspellings, repetitions, and general slovenliness that editors and scholars, from that day to this, have been wracking their brains in an effort to make it legible. Most of the doubtful passages have yielded to research and common sense, but a stubborn nub of them remains which I have had to guess at or give up altogether. They are indicated in the Notes.

The imperfections of Contreras' copy and certain manifest weaknesses in the book itself have led me to take several editorial liberties with the text. Since the original title has no meaning for the English reader, I have invented the present one, which is more descriptive of its content and purpose. From the earliest printed edition to the present, editors have been aware of this problem and have solved it by adopting the title of Boccaccio's famous tirade against women and calling it *El Corbacho* (*The Scourge*), which they further amplified by tacking on the subtitle *Reprobación de amor mundano*, probably borrowed from the *De amore* of Andrea Capellanus. In this they have done the Archpriest an injustice, allowing the reader to infer that his book is derivative in its entirety. Superficially, to be sure, it is derivative, but the substance and the style of it are his, inimitably his.

Another thing: the Archpriest plainly indicates

at the end of Part Three that his book is finished. Just why he felt impelled to add a long and insufferably dull treatise on astrology is a mystery. It is not part of his original plan and it introduces a logic-chopping Schoolman's style utterly at variance with his usual free-swinging colloquialism. So I am sparing the reader (and myself) that part of the book. If the reader is curious to know what he is missing, let him turn to Part Three, Chapter Six, where he will find a small but adequate sample of it. Again, in the original the Archpriest included the chapter "Of Matrimony" in his treatment of the phlegmatic man. I have made it a separate chapter, as it deserves. Further to tidy things up and to preserve continuity, I have reversed the order of appearance of the phlegmatic man and the melancholy man at the end of Part Three.

Finally, it is likely that the reader of today will boggle at the Archpriest's meandering and fusty attack on the general problem of sin, to which he devotes the whole of Part One. I could not omit it without damaging the structure of the book, but the reader may be well advised to turn at once to Part Two, where the Archpriest gets down to business, so to speak, and pick up the general argument later.

In the tantalizing and thoroughly enjoyable task of putting the Archpriest into English I have had the generous help of my colleagues, Professors E. B. Place, H. R. W. Smith, and Luis Monguió, and, as always, that of my eagle-eyed and sympathetic critic, my wife. To all of them my warm thanks.

LESLEY BYRD SIMPSON

JHUS

THIS BOOK WAS COMPOSED BY ALFONSO MAR-
TINEZ DE TOLEDO, ARCHPRIEST OF TALAVERA,
AT THE AGE OF FORTY YEARS. IT WAS COM-
PLETED ON THE FIFTEENTH DAY OF MARCH, IN
THE YEAR OF OUR SAVIOUR JESUS CHRIST, 1438.
WITHOUT BENEFIT OF BAPTISM LET IT BE
CALLED, WHITHERSOEVER IT MAY BE BORNE,
The Archpriest of Talavera

⌐ Prologue

In the name of the Holy Trinity, Father, Son, and Holy Ghost, three persons and one true God, Maker, Arranger, and Composer of all things, without whom nothing can be well done, well said, begun, half done, or finished, and having as mediator, intercessor, and advocate the humble and spotless Virgin Mary, I, unworthy, Alfonso Martínez de Toledo, Bachelor at Canon Law, Archpriest of Talavera, and chaplain to our sovereign lord and King of Castile, Don Juan (whom God preserve for long and fruitful years), have undertaken to write a brief compendium in Spanish for the instruction of those who may desire to read it and, having read it, to remember it, and, having remembered it, to put it into practice. This I do especially for those who have not yet trod the ways of the world, or drained its bitter cup, or tasted its sour dishes. I do not write or speak for those who have done so, for their knowledge will suffice to protect them from evil-doing.

My book is divided into four principal parts. In the first I shall condemn worldly love. In the second I shall treat somewhat of the ways of wicked women. In the third I shall do the same for the various complexions of men: what they are and what virtues such men have for loving or being loved. In the fourth* I shall conclude by exposing the vulgar error of those who believe in fate, luck, fortune, signs, and planets, an error condemned by our Holy Mother Church, as well as by those whom God endowed with sense, intelligence, and natural judgment. This I do to correct those who say that if they have sinned in love, their fate or fortune made them do so.

With this purpose in mind I have gathered together certain notable sayings of a Doctor of Paris, Juan de Ausim[1] by name, who wrote somewhat of the love of God and reprobation of the worldly love of women, and how Our Lord God, whose might is above all mundane and transitory things, should be loved, not because of the perpetual punishment that He will visit upon the world, but for pure love and delight in Him, who is so great and good that He alone is worthy of being loved. Indeed, He so commanded us in His first law: *Thou shalt love thy God, thy Creator, and thy Lord above all things.* Therefore, since He so commanded us, we must love only Him and leave behind us and forget the transitory things of this world, because by truly loving Him, and loving His infinite glory, there is no doubt that we shall attain it forever and ever. If, on the contrary, we cast aside His love, and desire and love the vain things of this world, and forsake the infinite Creator for the finite and slavish creature, there is no doubt that he who does so will be condemned to eternal torment. Woe to the unlucky

---

* Omitted in the translation.

wretch who, merely to satisfy his willful appetite which quickly passes, loses the everlasting glory of Paradise which endureth forever!

Ah, if the wretched man or woman only understood the meaning of that word *forever!* And what it means to attain glory or pain in the next world forever and ever! Ah, if they would only think upon this a single hour of the day, why, I doubt they could commit any evil act whatever! But our hearts are more set these days upon doing evil, even though we know we shall suffer for it (for man does indeed suffer for his wickness), than upon doing good in the hope of glory (for man will assuredly attain glory by doing good). It will, therefore, be a useful and holy deed to correct those things which are the cause of our evil-doing, for more and more nowadays we beg forgiveness for our sins, but, in expectation of pardon, continue our wicked lives without visible improvement and without fear of just retribution. And one of our most common sins is disorderly love, especially love of women, whence follow discords, murders, deaths, scandals, wars, loss of our goods, ruin of our bodies, and, much worse, the loss of our miserable souls, because of this abominable carnal sin and disorderly love.

The world has fallen into such a state of decay that nowadays the beardless youth and the old man full of years alike love women madly. And what of the tender maiden who loses her good name in the world because of the malicious gossip that makes her out to be older in sin than she really is? Or the old woman in the shadow of the grave, deserving to be burned alive! Everyone knows about love these days and, worse, they practice it, so much so that the world is plainly going to ruin. Once upon a time a youth of twenty-five hardly knew what love was, nor did a maiden of twenty; but what one sees today is too shameful to relate. And so, as I have said, it seems to me that the end of the world is at hand. Privileges, laws, friendship, kinship, and neighborliness are no longer a deterrent for this sin, and everything is headed straight for the burning. How many marriages, for example, are unlawfully broken these days because of this sin, as a husband abandons his own wife for another? And so, seeing so much evil and harm, I have set myself to write and speak a little of this matter, exposing in sermons certain things that are practiced today, as you will hear, repeating, as I said, the sayings of that Doctor of Paris who compiled a brief compendium in reprobation of love for the instruction of a friend of his, a youth much given to it, seeing him tortured and vexed by the love he bore his mistress, who could more accurately be called his cruel enemy and torment of his life. He began by admonishing him and giving him to understand that only the love of God is true love and that the love of all else is vanity, wind, and a mockery. He demonstrated his teaching, moreover, by actual experience and natural argument, open to all who will read and understand, that is, about wicked women, their faults, vices, and blemishes, what they are and, in some degree, how many they are.

At this point the author ceases, for they are numberless and cannot be described, because he who has to do with wicked women will see in them things undreamed of, never written, seen, or known. And I say the same of wicked, perverse, and accursed men, worthy of suffering the fires of hell for the single act of dishonest love of women, mad, senseless, and bestial—which is more appropriate than calling it love. This I write with the express protestation that if anything should be well said in this compendium, or if anyone should be improved by it, let it be in the service of Him we are obligated to love truly and none other. If, on the other hand, anything should be said or written here of the vices and evil lives of men and women, let it not be laid to my desire to detract, vilify, or speak evil, or defame, but rather to my desire to correct those men and women in whom the said vices are in continual exercise and use, and to praise the virtuous in their virtues, for if evil were not castigated, virtue would not be recognized. To speak ill of a bad man is to praise the good man. Hence I believe that he who wastes his substance and person in mad love has little regard for his good name and reputation, and that he who eschews this false and insidious love will achieve great merit, if he can control himself. But he who because of age or impotence is incapable of love and eschews it, let it not be said of him that he eschews love, but rather that love eschews him. He who has the power to sin and sins not is more pleasing to God than he who, although he would like to sin, is unable to do so. Certain men and women, therefore, sensing at times their own inconstancy and lack of resistance to this sin, say: "O Lord, take away my desire, since Thou hast taken away my power!" This because they would sin. Or, on the other hand: "O Lord, give me the power, since Thou gavest me the desire which caused me to sin!"

Shun continuous companionship and frequent intercourse, man with woman, woman with man, and idle, obscene, and filthy words that incite to evil, and all idleness and association with dishonest, lecherous, and evil-speaking company, and lower your eyes and let them not rest upon every person who happens to attract them. These are things that will remove much evil-doing and cause you to scorn that vain love which kills the soul as well as the body, or kills the body and condemns the soul to perpetual punishment. And so I will begin by explaining the most important thing, that is, how the love of God alone is proper love, and none other.

PART ONE

CHAPTER ONE

⌐ *How he who madly loves is displeasing to God*

First, I will state a proposition that none can gainsay, to wit, that no man can be pleasing to God who gives himself up to worldly love, because Our Lord God, in the Old Testament as well as the New, condemns it and commands the punishment of all those who are guilty of fornication and lechery, excepting only those who are joined together in holy matrimony, for these are innocent of mortal sin, that is, if they perform the said act properly and within the said order of matrimony for the increase of mankind. But He commands that those be punished who commit the said act through unbridled appetite.

I ask you, then, whether a thing can be called good which is done against the will of God? Oh, how many heartaches, and how much bitterness of spirit, there are in what we hear, learn, read, and see each day, that is, in vile, obscene, and horrible acts of lechery committed in sundry forms! To think of losing the glory of God for a fleeting moment of unrestrained appetite, vile, filthy, and horrible! Oh, how luckless and infamous is he, deserving to be numbered among the beasts and worse, who for a brief carnal pleasure forfeits enduring bliss and condemns himself to the pains of hell!

Think, therefore, my brother, and with your fine understanding consider, what honor should be accorded him who, scorning his Lord and heavenly King, and scorning His commandment, gives himself to the devil, that enemy of God and His law, for a blind and wretched woman, or for his desire for her! You may well reflect, my friend, that if Our Lord God had desired that this sin of fornication might be committed without sin, He would not have ordained the celebration of marriage, for it is clear and plain that people would multiply more rapidly by committing fornication than otherwise. Consider, therefore, the madness of those who for a moment of carnal pleasure forfeit that eternal life which Jesus Christ Our Saviour redeemed with His own blood and saved from perdition. Therefore, I say unto you that it will be in the confusion of his soul and the shame of his face, and, even more, an affront to Almighty God, if a man follows the willful dictates of his miserable appetite and goes against the will of God, and so living loses what He promised you (although you deserve it not), as I have said already, shedding His own blood which will rise up and demand God's justice of you! O cruel judgment, how little considered and less pondered! Let him who can or will, therefore, bear in mind that only the love of God is true love, since He died for love of you. And then you would repay Him by loving another!

CHAPTER TWO

⌐ *How he who loves his neighbor's wife
offends God, himself, and his neighbor*

I will now offer you another and better argument, the
second in order, explaining why lovers of women
and the world should fly such love, for they cannot fail to offend their neighbor by desiring, with
false love, to possess his wife or his daughter, his
niece or his cousin, dishonestly. And if you do such
a thing, knowing as you do that it is wrong, do you
not, then, desire for yourself what you should not
desire for your neighbor? In so doing you commit three sins: first, you transgress God's commandment; second, you wrong your neighbor; third, you
ruin and destroy your body and lose your soul.
There is even a fourth: you ruin the unfortunate
woman who believes in your love, for she will lose
her life if the affair is discovered, because her husband
will kill her justly, either suddenly and untimely,
or with poison. Or the father will kill his daughter, or the cousin his cousin, or the brother his sister,
as we see happen every day. And if she is a virgin
and loses her virginity, and they wish to marry her
off, why, then they go about madly seeking to do
that which never could or can be done, namely, to
make a virgin out of one who has been defiled. This
is the source of many evils. At times, even, they have
recourse to charms to keep her husband from having
carnal intercourse with her. And if by chance the
said virgin becomes pregnant by her mad lover, then
off they go to find some way of getting rid of the
baby, dead!

Oh, how many evils of this kind follow among virgins, as well as among widows, nuns, and even married women when their husbands are absent: among married women through fear of their husbands, among widows and nuns through fear of dishonor, among unmarried girls through grief, for they know that if they are discovered they will forfeit marriage and honor! But the truth is that the best woman as well as the worst loses so much by giving herself up to mad love that death would be life for her, whether it is discovered or not. I know, moreover, that it is quite impossible to hide it. It would, in fact, be idle to try to exhaust this subject. Consider, therefore, the many evils that unbridled love causes and brings about, especially since there is a divine commandment against it. I say further that, even though there were no such commandment, you should still avoid it for the profit and well-being of your neighbor. Besides, you should not desire for him what you would not desire for yourself, because without the love of his neighbor a man would live but a short while in this miserable world.

CHAPTER THREE

How love is the cause of death, violence, and war

My third point is that none should pursue the love of women or desire it, for because of such love we see friendships broken daily, and quarrels between lovers and their mistresses, between brothers and sisters, fathers and sons; and we see mortal enmities arise, and many deaths occur, and an infinity of other evils. Read the ancients and listen to men still living. Consider well that there is no man alive, however close a friend he may be, or how cordially he may esteem you, even a close kin—and to this rule there is no exception, be he cousin, nephew, brother, or even, I say, your father—who, when he discovers that you are in love with his mistress, or show her any affection, does not forthwith conceive for you in his heart a mortal dislike, hatred, and rancor. From that moment he will strive to do you hurt in every way he can, publicly or privately, according to his station; for a man will openly attack his equal, but dares not act against his betters except in secret. And this is the source of many dark deeds and Italian tricks, and of murders and stabbings, and of so many other things that it would be tedious to recount them.

Woe to the unlucky wretch who for a moment of carnal pleasure and his unbridled love for an inconstant woman would dishonor his friend, make of him an enemy for life, and lose him forever! From such a man, therefore, as from a brutish beast and enemy of the human race, all persons of judgment should fly, as from a venomous serpent or rabid dog that poisons everyone it bites or touches. What is more useful or profitable for a man to have than faithful friends whom he can trust? According to Cicero the Roman, neither water, fire, nor money is more necessary to a man than his friend, loyal and true, who, if such a one is discovered among a thousand, is to be cherished above all treasures. There is nothing to be compared with him, nor can anything be found. On the other hand, many, many are called friends, upon whom the name is thrust, as well as the deeds, but the name lacks truth, for their friend-ship vanishes in time of need; it has the appearance but lacks the substance. A true friend is proved in time of trouble and is then the more loyal and kind, for, as the ancient saying has it: "Whilst thou art rich, oh, how many friends thou hast! But, when the weather changes and the sky is overcast, alas, how alone thou shalt be!"

The worth of a true friend is well brought out by Tully, in a book of his called *De amicitia*. In his friendship, then, you will know what kind of friend you have. Verily, the name of friend should be withheld from that friend of yours, whatever or whoever he may be, and he should be held in small esteem, who, to satisfy a bit of vain appetite, loses God and ruins his friend. Such a one should never have shown his face among men, or even have been born! Other sins kill the body, but this one kills the body and damns the soul as well. The body, in lech-ery, suffers in all its five natural senses. First, a man loses his sight and his sense of smell, for he can no longer smell as he used. He loses his taste and even his power of eating, entirely. His hearing fades and it seems to him that he has bumble bees in his ears. His hands and his whole body lose the strength they once had and begin to tremble. All three powers of the soul are disturbed, for he has hardly any under-standing or memory left, and cannot remember to-morrow what he does today. He can no longer exer-cise the seven virtues: faith, hope, charity, prudence, temperance, fortitude, and justice, and thus he is turned into an irrational beast. Worse, the vile act of lechery causes the wretch to become callous in sin, not only in this one but in others by contamination, and he grows old in them. Many, therefore, are damned who die suddenly when they least expect it or think they are most secure, and they say: "Today or tomorrow I will mend my way, or get rid of such and such a vice." Thus by putting things off from day to day the poor wretch ends in the arms of Satan, which is the worst fate of all, it is needless to say. So not without reason does the Divine Authority cry out to us, saying: "There is no graver crime than fornication, for it leads man to perdition."

CHAPTER FOUR

How he who loves is in his loving altogether fearful

There is yet another argument which should persuade the wise to shun mad love, for he who loves binds himself and kills himself, and from a master becomes a slave, because he imagines that everyone he sees is usurping his love. Thus with the slightest suspicion his whole heart is disturbed and turned upside down, and he fears every word, every movement, every association with another. A lover is so delicate that he is always fearful and frightened, and thinks that the loved one is angry with him and is casting her eyes upon another. So the poor fool loses his taste for food and cannot sleep, and has no pleasure or amusement, for his single thought is that he is being deceived by the one he loves, because he loves and is not loved.

And if he should see another speak with her, even though it be his own brother, he forthwith assumes

that the other is stealing her from him, or is per-
suading her to leave him, or is deceiving her and
wants her for himself. Then his heart is consumed
with rage and he is at war with himself, especially
since there are certain flighty women whose eyes
roam about in all directions and who smile at everyone, because they would be desired, loved, and es-
teemed by many, and bestow their fruits like the
vineyard of the Lord: who wants them not, harvests
them not; who would not enter, enters not. So the
poor wretch lives, and living, dies, and dies each day
he lives. And he thinks that there is no treasure in
the world more to be prized than his ladylove, nor
would he give a fig for any other. Truly, he who
loves suffers this evil in his person and estate, and
says he is fortunate only in the enjoyment of his
love, and it never occurs to him that misfortune can
touch him. If, on the other hand, he is not sure of
his love, all things, it seems to him, go wrong, and
no one can get a friendly gesture or cheerful glance
from him, as though he were changed and trans-
muted into a different species.

Who is so mad and out of his mind that he will
yield up his will to another, or give over his liberty
to one unworthy, and become the slave of a woman
of little sense, and tie himself hand and foot, so that
he is no longer his own master—all this against the
words of the wise man who said: "He who can be
his own master, let him not sell himself, for liberty
and freedom are not to be bought for gold?" This
is an ancient saying that the Archpriest of Hita put
into his treatise. Such a man should in shame with-
draw himself from public view, like the man who
sold himself to someone or other, knowing it was
an enemy who intended to kill and mock him in the

end, for no man can be sure he will find constancy in the love of women, however handsome he may be, but it would be useless to try to persuade him, and to insist upon it would be a waste of time.

CHAPTER FIVE

⌐ *How he who loves hates his father and mother, his kin and friends*

I say further that I would prefer to have you love a woman who is not the wife of a friend. Rather, let her be unknown, or even a stranger. I say that a friend cannot know that another is his friend until he sees that the other's love is so strong that he would not betray him for anything in the world, but this takes a long time to prove. On the other hand, there is also harm in loving a woman who does not belong to an acquaintance or friend, for he who loves this woman, whoever she may be, thinks of nothing but ways to serve and please her, and, abandoning his love for his father and mother, kin and friends, who chide him for his love, he considers them all to be his enemies—this only to please his ladylove.

Even so, his hold on her amounts only to this: that when she sees another whose looks she likes better she will leave him in the air. And do not think that in this matter you will encounter greater faithfulness than did the ancients, who were experts in this science, or madness, rather. Read well what happened to Adam, Samson, David, Goliath, Solomon, Virgil, Aristotle, and others worthy of mention for their wisdom and natural judgment, to say nothing of an infinity of youths, dead or living.

Therefore, to expect constancy in a woman's love is as foolish as trying to empty a great river with a basket or very coarse sieve. So then, if this fellow will not take the example of others, or accept the teachings of his elders and those wiser than he, or learn by his own experience, how worthy is he to be abhorred and mocked at by men and his friends, who will say to him: "Oh, you unbridled colt! Your reins are loose. Run as far as you like until you fall down never to get up again!" For mettlesome and fervent lovers always run so fast that they fall headlong.

CHAPTER SIX

How lovers, loving, lose the respect of others

I have yet another argument, very contrary and indeed inimical to love, that is, we see that love brings about a great shrinking of one's estate, and that many have fallen, and are still falling, into deep poverty because of their mad love, freely giving, neglecting their commerce and property, and are now sunken and diminished in their estates. And often we see lovers dissipate their wealth in gifts just to display their great liberality to their mistresses; but in their own houses or elsewhere God knows how closefisted they are! They give where they should not and fail to give where they should. They are, therefore, prodigal and not liberal or generous —all this from love.

It even happens that a lover will give his mistress what is not his, and to get it from God or His saints,

by hook or by crook, he will do things he should
not do and expose himself to such dangers that it
would be a good thing for him to give up his mad
love altogether. Imagine a rich man wasting his
money on such a love and having his mistress learn
that he is now poor, not regaling her as he used, and
she insulting him, as we see every day! What do you
think of that? How painful it is, how harrowing, to
see this fellow, for the whole world turns dark for
him, green turns white, vermilion black, and purple
yellow! And I believe that in his desperation he
would not hesitate to commit any crime whatever
to recover if he can his misspent wealth, making no
mention now of his mistress, for the loss of his estate
is more painful to him than the loss of his mad
beauty. God help us! There are married men who
give their wives and families an evil time, and con-
sume their substance with mistresses and, when their
money is gone, have their mistresses jeer at them.
And so they go back to their houses and their proper
wives, moaning and cursing, with their tails between
their legs! How they suffer, having lost their love as
well as their goods! How they weep and roar about
the house! Sometimes like madmen they run away
to foreign parts, leaving their wives and children in
poverty. And now their wives face ruin and become
prostitutes to support themselves and their children!
And if the husband stays at home and does not abandon his wife, he must hold his tongue and put up
with it, pretending not to see, keeping out of the
way, and consenting.

This is what comes of mad and unbridled love, for
there is not a lover in the world who does not try to
get money wherever he can, in order to support his

mistress and keep his mad one happy—not only her, but the woman who covers them, and the messenger, and the procuress, and the woman who offers her house for their madness and sin, and the servant of the servant of her cook. Thus he must spend money in all directions, according to the place, and the rank and habits of his person. In short, he who loves must not only give to his mistress, but must keep a hundred others happy, even the neighbors, and work for them, also their neighbors' wives, so that they will not see what they see, or hear what they hear. So many tribulations are in store for the wretch who loves, not counting the infinity of dangers to which he must expose himself day and night, that it would be quite impossible to describe them, so many and so varied are they. And, after all, what good does it do him, if he is held in such contempt that no one gives a fig for him? For what will be the reputation of him who exposes himself to the said dangers and evils for the sake of a love that is neither enduring nor constant, and who refuses to heed the teachings of others, wiser, older, and more worthy than he? And what good does it do the wretched lover or his mistress, even though he achieves his love and gains the whole world, if his unlucky soul must spend eternity in lasting torment?

CHAPTER SEVEN

How many go mad from loving

A further argument against love is very strong; that is, a lover who loves immoderately makes his body suffer in this life and condemns his soul to torment in the next. Tell me, my friend, how many have you seen or heard of who loved in this world whose life was not made up of pain and suffering, worry, sighs, and vexations, sleeplessness, lying awake all night, lack of appetite, fretting, and, even worse, many of them dying of this evil and others going mad, and if they die their souls go to everlasting torment, not to mention their corporeal pain and suffering for two, three, or twenty years? Well then, what good does his love do the wretched lover, or his mistress, if he accomplishes his love, or even gains the whole world, and his soul must suffer perpetual torment in the other? So I say unto you, my friend, that he is accursed who loves a woman more than himself and who invites damnation for a brief pleasure, as I have said many times already, especially if he does so knowingly, after having been warned, and follows his desire, saying: "Kill, for the king will pardon!"

CHAPTER EIGHT

How chastity and continence are noble virtues in God's creatures

In this argument I shall demonstrate that love should be avoided, for there is no doubt that chastity and continence are very great and chosen virtues, just as lechery and the pleasures of the flesh are ugly and abominable vices. One of the things that a man should most cherish in the world is his good name and reputation, that he may be counted among the virtuous and not numbered among the vicious of blackened name. For neither man nor woman can enjoy a good name or wear a crown of virtue if it is not accompanied by continence and chastity, pleasing to God. Know also that virtues and vices, being contrary to each other, cannot reside in the same person, for the good man is not bad, nor the bad man good, although the bad can turn good and the good bad, and although during the time he is good he is not bad, and so on. I say further that in the old as in the young, in the cleric as in the layman, in the knight as in the squire, in the grown man as in the beardless youth, in man as in woman, honesty is the sister of shame, and chastity the mother of continence. And if these things reside in them, they are as much to be praised as their opposites are to be condemned.

I hold that in any man or woman, however exalted their rank, it is an ugly and unchaste thing to love, worthy of vituperation among honest and sensible men, for I believe it to be a great defect in man or woman, save in honest matrimony, where all honest love has its place. Tell me, my friend, what is your reason for wishing to love so madly, since in the eyes of God and man such love is held to be wicked and blasphemous? All you accomplish, by scorning God and losing your honor in the world, is to forfeit your good name and get yourself considered a brutish beast. Even a woman, however high her station, once it is learned that she is indulging in mad love, is held in scant renown by others. I say further that even the woman of low estate, even though she becomes the king's mistress, will never enjoy the reputation in the republic that she formerly enjoyed. Consider, then, how firmly a woman should deny her favors to everyone, for even as the king's mistress she is held to be as wicked as if she were sleeping with a baseborn tanner. I say this for those who think themselves lucky when they are taken up by a liberal lover, or by one of high estate.

Oh, mad and delirious women! Do they not know that by such they are soonest cast off and jeered at, by great and mean alike, and that the love of such is a mockery, a madness, a delusion, and a waste of time? If in men, because they are men, the vile act of lechery is somewhat tolerated, it is not thus with a woman who, in the very instant in which she commits such a crime, is held by all to be a wicked woman, and will be so held so long as she shall live. She cannot redeem herself, as can a man, by living a virtuous life, for a man, however much he has indulged in this sin, once punished and corrected, is praised for his mending and his sin is not held against him in the same degree as a woman's is against her, for her sin is perpetual, while a man's is transitory. Think well, therefore, upon this love, in man or woman, and take to yourself whatever pertains to you in this lesson.

CHAPTER NINE

How love causes many to perjure themselves and commit crimes

There is another reason why love is properly condemned by those who rightly reflect upon it. In the world there is no evil or crime which does not arise from it, for, as I have said, murders, adulteries, and lies have their source in love, for the lover often commits them in order to please or deceive his mistress, since his vows are not properly to be called vows, but rather lies. And thefts? Consider whether or not they are committed in many ways, one man stealing to give to another, the servant stealing from his master, the son from his father, and the husband secretly stealing from his wife in order to regale his mistress, giving her bad nights, bad days, bad breakfasts, and bad suppers. And if his wife learns of it and casts it up to him, then you should see how she has to pay for it in her goods and person! The husband gives to his mistress what belongs to his wife, and to his wife beatings and kickings and cuffings, and endless misery, until she leaves his bed and at last leaves him, as I have said already.

Consider well what love does, for doubt not that bearing false witness is often the effect of it. In the whole world there is no kind of lying that lovers do not employ and shamelessly make use of, if they have need of it. Anger proceeds from love, as is notorious and manifest to all men, when one does not do entirely or partly what a lover wishes, or does not applaud his appetite. In sum, all evils have their origin in dishonest love. I say further that there is no man, if you will closely observe the women of his household, however dedicated they may be to the service of God, who can keep the whip hand over them in affairs of love, as we see by experience every day. Many of these women, to be sure, even though they are in love, do not put it into practice, because they are held back, at times by fear of their kin, at times by chastity and shame. Love is also the cause of our worshiping strange gods and of idolatry, for even Solomon could not refrain from idolatry because of his mistress. If this could happen to so wise a man, what will become of you, poor wretch, since he whom God made the wisest of the wise thus sinned because of love? Who, then, will protect us who, compared with him, are unworthy even of being called men? And what I told you of Solomon I could repeat about other wise and valiant men. So, my friend, when you see a green and flourishing tree withering away, it is a sign that it is ready for the burning and is good for nothing else, and that it will yield no more fruit. Fly, therefore, the love of those from whom so many evils proceed, and love God who is the source of all good.

CHAPTER TEN

How the greater a man's ardor in lechery is, the greater is his repentance once it is accomplished

There is another argument against a man's yielding to love, if you will listen carefully, and that is that in any mad bout of love whatever, the longer this sin of fornication continues, the greater will be his repentance. To him who will consider this vile and filthy sin it is a notorious and palpable fact that however hot his fire is at the beginning of it, so much the greater will be his sudden repentance when it burns itself out. So true is this that there is no man in the world who after the act is not immediately sorry and repentant, and who during the act is not in pain. I say further that he is vexed by his own turpitude and filthiness, and his stomach turns, so to speak, at his lasciviousness, dishonest, vile, and filthy. Even so he will not hesitate to fall into it again forthwith and frequently because of his weak understanding and his lack of judgment and natural sense, or because of his willfulness in yielding to his appetite, thus becoming a slave when he could be master, as I said above.

Therefore I say unto you that so grave is this sin of carnality that even those who are united in God's ordained matrimony indulge themselves so excessively that they can hardly avoid committing venial sin. Indeed, so very many married couples sin so mortally in it that they respect no obligatory feast day, time, season, or even hour; nor do they observe the conditions and order of matrimony. Rather, the husband loves his wife, and the wife her husband, so unrestrainedly that they violate the law and institution of matrimony which should have the single chaste purpose of begetting children and the observance of the faith and the sacraments. But they forget all this and love each other madly in the delight and uses of the flesh. This is why David said: "Lord, I was begotten in iniquity and in sin did my mother conceive me." So, my friend, if in matrimony ordained by God you cannot avoid sinning, how much greater must be that same sin committed outside matrimony, against the precepts of God and His commandment! You who love, therefore, love in such wise that you will be beloved of God.

CHAPTER ELEVEN

⌐⁴ *How the priest and even the layman are destroyed by love*

Here is another argument that should persuade you to shun dishonest love, and it is that I have never seen an ecclesiastic (nor have you, for that matter, nor will you ever hope to see one) who has succumbed to dishonest love and won benefices or honors in God's Church. On the contrary, those who have succumbed and yielded to unbridled love have been ruined and will continue to be ruined, to their great shame, thinking to love a woman who does not and never could love them. For there is no woman, of whatever station she may be, who loves an ecclesiastic for any purpose other than to get something from him, such is the insensate greed of women to acquire and possess, and to go about in their mad finery vaingloriously. This is the reason they pretend to love them, but love them not. For example, there is not a woman in the world who does not hate ecclesiastics worse than poison, insulting them, scolding them, and gossiping about them, and this holds true for women who have got something from them, as well as for those who have not. And from this rule I do not except the laity, even though they are the sons of priests, for their mistresses never cease from vexing them, demanding presents and begging loans.

Furthermore, I ask what kind of sacrifice does he think he is making to God who by fraud or deceit, or by some other device, gets something, great or small, from an ecclesiastic? Even among gentlemen,

burghers, citizens, councilmen, justices, and others
of more or less consequence, there are lovers who
lose their honors and offices, and deny justice, because they are mad with love. Among the people
they are not counted as men, as you will see by
experience. For who will be put to govern others
who cannot govern himself? And who will be honored by the people who does not honor himself?
Who will favor him who fails to favor himself? And
who will help him who is bent upon his own destruction? And I say the same of women, whatever
their station may be. Let him who loves, therefore,
consider whom he loves and what profit there is in
madly loving, and he will not succumb if he thinks
before he acts.

CHAPTER TWELVE

*How he who loves is diligent in nothing
but his love*

Another argument against love is this: there is not
a single lover who is diligent in anything whatever save in those things that concern his love, for
in other things, his own affairs as well as his neighbor's, it is the same to him whether they are ruined
or prosper. I say further that he will listen to nothing, or bend an ear, except to what is said of his
mistress. In this he puts all his vigor, all his heart,
all his will. To listen to other things is death to him
and an unbearable annoyance. But if you speak to
him of his love for days and nights on end, he will
not be bored, even though he sleeps not a wink. And
if a friend has need of him and talks to him for a

whole hour, he will understand not a single word, for his disordered brain is occupied only with her he loves. The same is true of women. You see, therefore, how love disturbs the heart and weakens the will, and how this lasting fire of love never permits him who loves to rest or repose.

CHAPTER THIRTEEN

↱ *Of the evil thoughts that come to him who loves*

Love should be abhorred for yet another reason, which is this: that you should consider and know, as you must, that Almighty God is the source of blessed chastity, the beginning, the middle, and even the end. Monstrous Satan, on the other hand, is the head and counselor of lechery and shameless love, for he is the mortal enemy of the salvation of mankind. Therefore, in consideration of the authors of virtue and vice, we should cling to the safer, who is Jesus Christ, son of the humble Virgin Mary, in whose company salvation is certain. How blind is he who out of perversity fails to obey God and serves the devil! It is true, to be sure, that that enemy of God, the devil Satan, promises very sweet things to those who have the bad taste to follow their willful appetites, and he says to them: "Do what you like, for God is merciful. However much you sin, there will be plenty of time to repent before the end and you will be saved."

Thus the accursed one fills the human heart with many thoughts, but he cannot tempt the spiritual heart, which is not of this world. And when, with

flattery and false promises, he has done his will, as
a reward he gives the poor wretch a cup of gall to
drink and unimaginable perpetual torment. He does
so because from the beginning of the world he has
been a traitor and a liar. Then, when his victim is
in pain and damned to torment, the victim himself
would have all others follow in his steps and suffer
with him, for misery loves company. Such is the
reward that Satan gives to those who serve and obey
him! And so true is this that he who serves him best,
and believes and obeys him, is repaid, after this miserable life, with more pain and torment. I say further that the devil is like a robber who attacks a
traveler upon the road and who, after the traveler
has given him all his money in order to preserve his
life and gain protection from other robbers and evil-
doers, leads the traveler through crooked paths and
delivers him into the hands of the very ones he
feared. And then, when the traveler is stripped, the
robber who guided him gets as his reward a share
of the spoils from the others.

How many lessons and examples could be drawn
from this evil that is so common today! Let the fine
intelligence of him who reads this (if God, without
whom all learning is worthless, has seen fit to give
him such) suffice him. Thus the devil sallies forth to
attack the traveler in this world, saying to him:
"What will you give me if I prolong your life and
make you rich and prosperous, and allow you to
avenge yourself upon your enemies?" Etc. So the
unlucky wretch gives the devil his soul, his most
precious possession, and denies his God who created
him, and takes the devil for a master. And the devil
leads him through strange paths, and by subtle, un-

known, and undreamed-of means lets him have the things he desires, and in the end carries him off to hell and into the power of the very enemies he had feared, and the devil is the first to torture him!

Our Lord does otherwise, for, although He does not promise good things and sweets in doubled quantities, He rewards and pays us infinitely better, for He is our path and our highroad, our truth, health, and life, and for that reason He gives us a more abundant reward than does his evil supplanter, the devil.

When the evil one can find no other way to entangle those who live in this sin, he fills their hearts with consuming and unbridled love, so that even though the unlucky wretch sees hell on one side and his mistress on the other, in the blindness of his spiritual eyes he will choose to have his way with her, which he will do, even if he dies and goes to hell for it. In the lives of the Holy Fathers you will read of one who gave the devil a deed to his soul written in his own hand, in which he denied Almighty God and took the devil for a master, and all this merely to possess the woman he loved and got in this fashion. But, through the entreaties and prayers of another holy father, and in spite of the devil, the deed was visibly returned to him, all the other devils weeping bitterly the while at the loss of his soul. I verily believe that wretches may be found today who would give themselves to the devil to possess their mistresses; but they pay too heavily, as we know, because for lack of chastity they deny their God and because of their lechery take the devil for a master, and lose everlasting glory. Consider, therefore, my friend, whether it is unreasonable to look askance at a love which promises gifts, and then afterward you have to play the tune and pay the piper into the bargain.

CHAPTER FOURTEEN

How love is the cause of deaths and other evils

Another reason you should eschew love is that an infinity of deaths and unnumbered wars ensue from it, and many peaces are broken, as I have said, because of unbridled love of women. Thus we see cities, castles, and villages destroyed by love, and we see many rich men ruined because of it. Many have suffered for this sin and have even lost what their ancestors had won by their virtues, and so true is this that it is the firm opinion of many, as experience proves, that more men have died from their foolishness in loving than from the sword in cutting. And many more die because of women than are put to death by the authorities in the public defense. How much, therefore, should love be abhorred, this unbridled love that brings so many evils!

CHAPTER FIFTEEN

How marriages are destroyed by love

Still more evils can be charged to love. Dishonest love breaks up marriages and, as I said above, unbridled love at times is the cause of a husband's leaving his wife, or the wife her husband, and those whom God has joined together under His law and commandment, and whom no one should separate, are parted when dissolute love appears, even though St. Paul said: "Those whom God hath joined let no man put asunder." I ask you, further, what are the consequences of this false and unbridled love? Why, frequently a husband or his wife will plot to remove the other from this life. In fact, we daily see how one will murder the other, with poison, or will contrive to have him or her put out of the way by the authorities, if the case admits of it. In this world a man should love none but his own good wife, and she her husband, because by the first law of matrimony they are joined together and considered to be of one flesh, for God commanded that a man, abandoning all others, shall have but one wife, and He says further: "A man shall give up his father and his mother for her and go with his good wife, and thus the two shall be made one flesh and one will."

You know, of course, that you cannot commit fornication with your own wife, that is, if you conduct yourself properly, and even if you do not, it is not deemed to be a mortal sin to yield to the gross appetites of lechery, but only a venial sin, if the purpose of matrimony is kept safe and inviolate. From such matrimony will issue your legitimate children, called the blessed fruit of it and the heirs of all your goods, by whom, after you shall have departed this life, your name and memory will be kept alive. And your errors, if indeed you shall have committed any, will be redeemed by these children of yours who will do good works in your name. The same will not be done with equal love by the children of fornication and accursed coitus, abortive, in law called spurious, in Spanish bastards, and in vulgar speech children of wicked whores.

From this last, three evils follow: loss of his good name by him who begot such a son, infamy of her who bore him, and the vilification of him so engendered, for it is a mark that he will never lose, even after death. Besides, such a son is deprived of his paternal heritage as a punishment for the accursed coitus. Moreover, he is ineligible for all temporal honors, and even the Church will never allow him to hold a benefice unless he is first legitimized by the pope, or by his bishop, who in this case may give him permission to hold a benefice or two, but not the ones he would choose for himself. The Holy Scriptures say, moreover, that the children of adultery are abominable in the sight of God. Well then, if all these things follow from unbridled love, and if we see no good thing come of it, who is the fool who would not fly from it as from a hellish enemy? Therefore, my friend, learn to preserve your chastity entire and to overcome and vanquish the unbridled appetites of this miserable flesh, and guard your body from the stain of sin, for the sake of Our Lord God.

But if by chance you say that you cannot suffer, or hold in check, or resist the desires of the flesh, I will give you some good advice by which you will overcome them, and with no great constraint avoid the delights of this sin. First, if you are tempted in your thoughts by it, do not go to sleep with them in your mind. Cross yourself and beat your breast, and go at once to seek a person with whom you can talk of some business or other, and thus you will drive such thoughts from you. Or call in a neighbor or friend, or some servant or man of your household, and talk with him, even though you have no desire to do so. Or dash out of your house like one who shouts: "Help! I'm being murdered!" And when you are outside talk with someone of the neighborhood in order to take your mind off its intention. Item: shun dishonest places, and the occasions and persons that you know are the cause of your temptation. And if you are in a place where women are and you find yourself tempted by them, leave it and seek other company. And if by chance you are suddenly assailed by this accursed fire of lechery, take care at least, if you lack the will to resist and you consent to it in your own mind, take care at least, I say, to see that the act is not consummated, for it is a great evil, and a grave sin and a grievous, willfully to commit such a sin. But if you then do consummate it, the sin is very grave indeed, so grave that it kills the soul and sickens the body, turning it heavier than lead.

I say, therefore, that if you will observe this rule a few times and resist the assault of lechery when it comes, in a very brief while you will be master of it in your whole will, holding its goadings as nothing. And if this fire attacks you while you are in bed, leap out. Do not sleep with such a thought in your mind, but leave your house forthwith, and when your body cools, your flesh will cease its urgings. Or, when the attack begins, drop to your knees and pray, saying: *Ego peccator confiteor Deo*. And beat your breast, and thus you will overcome your accursed desire.

I have a further piece of advice for you, which for God's sake accept, for it will give you much comfort and consolation. Shun and avoid at least seven principal things. First, avoid eating and drinking excessively of rich and precious dishes. Second, eschew immoderate drinking of undiluted wine, for it is an incitement to lechery, as we learn from canonical law, because wine deprives a man of his understanding and causes him to err and sin. In another place the Apostle says: "Do not get drunk upon wine, for in it is lechery," as you have heard it said of Lot and others and see every day by experience, which is the mother, counselor, and mistress of deeds. Third, do not sleep in a bed which is over-soft, with delicate sheets and coverlets. Fourth, do not wear fine shirts next your flesh. Fifth, do not remain where women are, even though they are your kin or sisters, lest by regarding them you are reminded of others whom you desire or would like to see, or lest you are tempted to sin with their maids and servants, or with friends of theirs who come to visit them, because this happens at times, even with ecclesiastics who consort with women, according to the Decretal *Inhibendum*, in the third book of the Decretals. Sixth, as I said above, avoid lending your ear to evil words of lechery which incite to every wickedness, and avoid all idleness. Seventh and last, always be doing something to take vain imaginings from your mind, as the Holy Fathers tell us in their lives and sermons. And let the devil always find you so busy that temptation will find no place in you—which is one of the most useful remedies for the said sin. Furthermore, my friend, know that the character of lechery is such that if a man pursues it and continues in it, he will be enslaved and vanquished by it; but, if he avoids and shuns it, he will soon banish it, and it will depart from him as a lost thing of little value.

I tell you, my friend, that if you will put into practice what I have said, it will never be possible for vile lechery to spot or besmirch you, for lechery is no more to be feared than a Jew or a Moor. Show a bold face to it at its first advance and it will run away at once, for it has no strength if it cannot tempt, and flies at the sight of a man of courage.

And now, since it is manifest to any wise man whatever what women are, more or less, and how it was through them that destruction came to the world and still endures, it is not fitting longer to speak of them. Let it not be said that he who composed this book was a woman, for if he had been, from honesty he would cease this evil-speaking. But it is well to attack the vices of wicked women so that by hearing it they will abstain from evil-doing —which is no less true of perverse men, as I have said above, for my intention is only to admonish them to abstain from dishonest love, if I can, God willing, for there is no service more agreeable to God. And if this sin in man or woman is not avoided, nothing in them can be said to be finished or perfect; but if they fly and avoid it, there is nothing that more readily excuses and conceals their other vices and shortcomings, for if men and women are quit of mad love, and remain quit of it, there is no evil or ill fame said of them that will be believed. So great is the virtue of continence that it is a cloak to cover many sins. Indeed, if anyone should speak ill of him who is continent, he does not have to make reply, for everyone will vouch for him in one voice.

Very wise is he, therefore, who, although a sinner, cultivates a virtue that will protect him from the devil and his evil-speaking minions. Moreover, even if he lacks other virtues, this one will make him clean, pure, and shining as the sun. Consider also that a person who is continent and modest has need to be liberal and openhanded, and be not surprised at this, for when a person is stingy, beggarly, and closefisted, all his virtues are held to be dead. And what I say applies no more to the temporal than to the spiritual, for, understand well this point, all the good things that the people might say of such a man they keep to themselves. As the Apostle Paul says: "Faith without works is dead." Thus a virtue unaccompanied by liberality and generosity is not held to be a virtue, and, since love is a vice and not a virtue, it is wisdom to shun it.

CHAPTER SIXTEEN

How he who gives himself to lechery loses his strength

Another argument against love and lovers is that the human body is greatly weakened thereby, and lovers who engage in warfare or other activities are not at all strong. Men are thus made weak in four ways. First, according to the doctors of medicine, lechery is the efficient and final cause of the weakening of the human body. Second, he who indulges in such pleasure loses his appetite in great part, and because of his ardor and burning dryness he takes to drink, for every violent movement causes heat, and heat is the cause of dryness, and both, dryness as well as heat, cause destruction. Wherever this dryness occurs it is necessary to prescribe the contrary to cure it, for opposites are cured with opposites, as Aristotle says. It is necessary, therefore, to temper the said heat by drinking a quantity of cold things. There are things, however, which appear to be cold but which, like wine, are very heating, for wine, however cold and pure it may be and however often it is drunk, is in itself heating; it burns the liver and inflames the body, so much so that the body hardly feels the cold. As the saying has it: *Garlic and wine are the poor man's comforters.* An empty stomach is upset by much drinking and cannot digest, and it necessarily follows that the propelling force of the stomach which sends its influences in great amount to the arteries, veins, and other agents of administration and distribution, is weakened and gives out. And so, since the stomach fails to supply the body with the nourishment which it is its duty to give, all its powers are weakened and diminished so much that the body loses its strength. Third, love and lechery deprive a man of his sleep, for he cannot sleep as he used and should, and deprived of sleep he spends his nights worrying, and worrying, he never rests, and never resting, he loses his joy. Now, since it is natural that loss of sleep causes indigestion, and that indigestion, as I have said, causes the loss of bodily strength, it follows that loss of sleep is the source of all sickness, as medical authorities have proved. A doctor of medicine called Joanicio says that sleep and rest are the restorative of animals and the natural virtue given them for their conservation and increase. Thus we may say that loss of sleep is a painful hardship in animals and weakens their natural powers, and that if this is true, it is also true that their bodily strength cannot remain at its full vigor. Fourth, love and lechery cause many ailments and shorten the life of man, making a man grow old before his time, causing his limbs to tremble, and, as I have said above, they disturb his five senses and destroy some of them, either partly or entirely. At times they drive him mad with worry, or else they deprive a man and woman both of their natural judgment and sense to such a degree that they do not know themselves, or where they are, or what has happened to them, or how it is they are alive.

Therefore, since unbridled love is the cause of so many bodily ills, it would be the part of wisdom to abandon it and give it no importance, although at times, to be sure, holding things to be of no importance is the source of much harm and confusion, for he who turns his back upon his enemy, dies at his hands. So then, for God's sake let us truly love in such wise, loving God alone, that we shall gain everlasting life.

CHAPTER SEVENTEEN

How the learned lose their learning through love

For yet another reason I advise you to give up love, for the man of law or the scholar, if he abandons himself to dishonest love, loses all wisdom and learning, because, however learned and wise he may be, if he yields to love and lechery, from that moment he loses all temperance and cannot abstain from it. Rather, I say, the more learned he is, once he has got himself involved in this practice, the less chance he

has to free himself, less even than the simple igno-
ramus, as I have said. Has anyone ever heard of a man
of more unparalleled wisdom than Solomon? Or one
who committed a greater piece of idolatry than he
did for his mistress? Aristotle, too, one of the wisest
and most learned men who ever lived, allowed himself to be saddled and bridled and cinched like a
donkey, and ridden by his mistress, who lashed his
rump the while! Who, then, should not renounce
love, seeing how mad love made an idolator and
slave of a great lord and king, and how a foolish
woman made of the wisest of men a bridled donkey,
going on all fours like a beast!

Let this be noted by all lovers, and it should suffice for all who meddle with love: Virgil, a man of
such learning that none has ever been known to sur-
pass him in science and magic, as you may read,
hear, and see in the books written about him—this
Virgil, then, do you not know that he was left hanging from a tower window in a basket, gaped at by all
the people of Rome, and only because he had boast-
ed that he was so wise that no woman could deceive
him? So a woman matched her presumptuousness
against his and, as she bragged, deceived him in fact,
for there is no wickedness in the world, past, present, or future, which a wicked woman has any diffi-
culty whatever in executing or putting into effect.

But here I should like to defend men a bit. They
are not deceived because of their learning, for, if a
man so desired, no woman could deceive him, although St. Augustine, to be sure, has some doubt
about this. But a man trusts a woman and, trusting
her, wishes to please her and allows himself to be
deceived by her—which is to err from disordered

willfulness rather than from ignorance. Women take
pleasure in such yarns and boast of the tricks that
the women of old played on the wisest men. Let us
speak no further here of the deceptions that men
suffered and will continue to suffer every day because of their mad love. The said Virgil did not
let the woman off unpunished, but repaid her hand-
somely, for by his magic art he extinguished in a
single hour all the fire in the whole city of Rome,
so that every man came to her to get fire from her
privy parts, but the fire that one got did not profit
the next and each had to do so for himself—this in
revenge for the dishonor she had brought upon so
wise a man.

You must know, moreover, as I believe you do,
that King David, a wise man above all wise men,
and a prophet of God above all prophets, had a mul-
titude of wives and concubines, and that he was
unable to satisfy his outrageous appetite even with
all of them, and they were as beautiful as a king
with all his power could command. So with evil
intent and unbridled willfulness he dishonestly loved
Bathsheba, the only wife of Uriah, a gentleman of
his who loved her. For the king had seen her in her
garden every day combing her hair and arraying
herself before his eyes, and she came daily to do so,
even exposing her breasts, although she pretended
that she did not know he was there, as many others
are in the habit of doing these days. And so the
king, not content with many, loved and coveted the
only wife of Uriah, and with her committed carnal
sin, or adultery, as it is called in canonical law—
which same he would not have committed had she

not desired it when she saw and sensed the beginning of the king's love, and had she not continued to come and array herself there as she did. Such was the cause of the dishonor and the death of her husband, as well as the death of many men who died because of the sin that David committed, for it pleased Our Lord that David's son Abalom should rise up against him and force him to fly from Jerusalem and commit fornication with his concubines in the sight of all the people. You will see, therefore, if you read further into the story, the great evil that the wife of Uriah caused, although David was not innocent either. And you will also see how much wickedness one woman is capable of, even today.

After the king had committed the said sin with the wife of Uriah, she gave birth to a boy, and the child died, and great was David's grief thereat. Nevertheless, still unsatisfied, David had the husband slain, sending him to Joab, the commander of his armies, with an order to put Uriah in the front rank, where he would be killed; for Uriah was a man of honor and knew that if King David should put him to such a test he could not long remain alive. You should understand, moreover, that David would not have had him slain if he had not done him such a great wrong by taking his wife and stealing her affections. But the king was uneasy lest Uriah, discovering such wickedness, should kill his wife and deprive David of her love, and lest Uriah, perhaps, moved to despair, should be disloyal to his king and lord. Thus it is that he who breaks faith with another cannot expect that other to be faithful to him, and this is especially true in the case of a lord's breaking faith with his vassal, lest the vassal kill his lord. And all this is the result of mad and unbridled love.

I say further that I knew in my day a great many men and women who saw a notable man of the king's household, perhaps the second most powerful man of Aragon and Sicily, Mosén Bernard de Cabrera by name, imprisoned by the king and queen in Sicily because he had done great wrong to his lord and king, disobeying him by possessing many castles and strong places—which is why he was imprisoned. So, in order to debase and dishonor him, they had a mistress of his whom he loved advise him to escape by a window of the tower where he was imprisoned, and then to lie with her and escape from her house —all this by order of the king, and she was pleased to obey. And he, little thinking she would betray him, believed her and took a rope that she sent him. His guard did not interfere and allowed him to file the lock of the window and open it. So at the first hour of the night he left by the window and began his descent from the tower. But half way down a strong open sweep net called a *jábeca* had been spread, with its fittings. And when he was in the net those who were at the window closed it and cut the ropes, and he was left hanging there with nothing to eat or drink until the next afternoon, when they released him. And all the townspeople and those from without came to see him where he was hanging, clad only in his shirt, like Virgil. Thus you see how false and fickle love causes even the wisest to fall. Let each man, then, consider his own actions and obey the adage which goes: *When you see your neighbor's beard being plucked, put your own to soak.*

CHAPTER EIGHTEEN

↱ How a woman's love is full of deceit

I should like to persuade you lovers with yet another argument, to wit, that this love which you seek so avidly you will never find in a woman, because there was never a man who loved a wife or mistress to excess who was loved by her. This is a rule that is well known by those who have tested it. But my pen, not to be the instrument of evil-doing, ceases at this point, because we know by experience that many women love best those who beat and mistreat them. Besides, a woman's thought is that she will get rich by loving and that he who loves her will shower gifts upon her. Her love has two motives: that which I have just mentioned, and a second, willful and carnal pleasure. In this latter case a woman cares not for a man's gifts, nor does a man for a woman's, but they are solely concerned with satisfying their appetite. And that is why you will see widows as well as wives take up with base, ugly, poor, luckless, and worthless men, crippled, one-armed or one-eyed, and even hunchbacks. And I say no more. When women love men of this kind they do so for two reasons. The first is that they are like bitch wolves, for cold and love cannot be kept out, and they get heated over the first one who happens by and would go to bed with him. Men do the same. The second is that a man is a glib talker, or he lives nearby, or it is because such foolish and worthless men frequent the places where women gather, and so, since they are not thought to be dangerous by the kin and friends of the women who should be looking after them, these fellows do much harm and

evil. The same holds true for idiots, or rascals who
are more than a little mad, for they are not guarded
against. Frequently, therefore, these fellows are the
fathers of the foundlings dropped at the church
door at matins.

There are other types of women who love and
desire such, and these fellows, to save them from
shame and ridicule, are as silent as a black girl at a
bath—this from love or fear: for love, in order not
to lose them and to have them at their disposal whenever they please. And women never take anything
from such, because they have nothing. Rather, they
give them gifts, either to stop their mouths or to
keep from losing them. The second reason for the
silence of these fellows is their fear that if a woman's
kin or friends should hear of it their lives would be
forfeit. This is why they keep silent and why their
women love them, as I have said—which would not
be true of men of higher station who would as soon
talk as not. Indeed, such make the rounds of the
squares and wineshops, boasting: "You did that, but
I did this; you have three mistresses, I four; you
sleep with queens, I with empresses; you with serving maids, I with gentlewomen; I with Peter's
daughter, you with Rodrigo's wife; I with María,
you with Eleanor; you go by night, I by day; you
enter by the door, I by the window; your go-between is So-and-so, my pimp is Rodrigo; you go at
twelve o'clock, I at one; your mistress gave you a
shirt, mine gave me a doublet; you slept with yours
alone, I with mine and two maids; yours gave you
rose water, mine gave me orange blossom water;
your mistress is very dark, mine very white; yours
is puny, mine buxom; yours is not beautiful, mine

is shapely and pretty. So, then, you come with me to see my mistress and I'll go with you to see yours, because you must have company to get the most pleasure out of love."

If a lover quarrels with his mistress, let him make peace. Or, if they get angry with each other, count it merely a spat between lovers, and let the go-between patch it up. Well, then, these fellows, what with their whispering and gossip, and ogling their mistresses shamelessly at weddings, in the square, at joustings and tournaments, at bullfights or at church, have no fear of kinsmen, friends, or husbands. So bold are they, indeed, that they commit dishonest acts with their mistresses, fearless of God, justice, and shame of the world, not like those other poor wretches. And this is why their mistresses at times come to hate them, however gallant they may be, and prefer a bird in hand to two in the bush, an ass that will carry them to a horse that will throw them.

Thus, as I have said, a woman's motive in love is to get and to possess, because that is her nature, for most women are avaricious and when they get their hands on something they never let go. They love temporal riches to a superlative degree, and to get money and keep it they put their minds and bodies to some very cunning uses, and in this they are most diligent and clever. I have never seen a woman refuse what was willingly offered her, or one who did not insistently demand what had not even been promised her, or one who, if by chance she had demanded something and it was not given her, did not forthwith cease from loving him who refused her. Not only that, but even if you should give her everything you own, and she sees that you have lost your wealth and estate, or if you should be brought low by some long sickness that prevents your frolicking with her as you used, then God help you! She will impose perpetual silence upon you and threaten you with her kinsmen. Or she will say that she no longer has the opportunity to please you. Or she will say that her people have learned of your affair and are keeping their eye on her and will not let her sleep where she did. Or that she cannot talk with you at her door or window and cannot leave the house. Nothing is as it was, since you do not frolic with her or regale her as you once did. How many women act in this way with no fear whatever! All the pleasures you once enjoyed are now denied you. Now that the clink of doubloons and florins is heard no longer and the gay times are over, it's off with you like a worn-out horse to the treadmill, or like a broken gambler to the rubbish heap! And do not think that you will ever find a woman, however much in love with you she may be, who, if another happens by with greater gifts and jewels for her, will not send you packing. So great indeed is her unbridled appetite for getting money and wealth, that a wicked woman will abandon all continence and chastity to acquire goods, jewels, finery, and riches.

I say further that if you have money and approach a wicked woman with your hands open, it will be very odd if you do not come away with your purpose accomplished, or at least a promise. But if you ask of a woman even the price of a pin you will be wasting your time and you will not see a smile on her face for ten or twenty days. However exalted your station may be, if you go to her with empty hands, you will never get her to consent. On the contrary, she will scream at you shamelessly: "What do you want, my friend? Get out and bad luck go with you!" And she will pretend she does not know you and has never seen you before. I tell you the truth, that, such is their wicked greed and unbridled avarice, evil women are all thieves in one degree or another. Their hands are smeared with honey and everything sticks to them. I say further that gifts, silver, jewels, or gold, or other precious things will bring low the highest of them, for gifts will break stones. And if this is so, how can weak flesh resist? I say, therefore, that you will not find a really poor woman among a thousand; nor can it be otherwise, so great is their burning desire to acquire and heap up riches, honors, estates, and finery. They would not be satisfied, indeed, with all the kingdoms and principalities in the world. This is their desire, for there is no serf who, if he should become a lord, would be recognizable; nor is there a vassal become a lord who does not turn cruel.

In this you will be able to recognize whether people come from good or bad stock, for a man who comes from good stock can hardly help showing it, even though he may not look the part; but the baseborn, or he of low estate and lineage, if fortune brings him wealth, estate, honor, and position, will immediately betray his origin, no matter how hard he tries to be different from what he is, as some are in the habit of doing. For the truth is that the offspring of a goat is going to bleat at some time or other, and that of an ass to bray, for such is their nature. For example, take two boys, one the son of a farmer, the other that of a gentleman, and let them be reared in a wilderness under the care and discipline of a man and his wife. You will see that the farmer's son will still be pleased with the things of village life, such as plowing, digging, and hauling firewood on asses; but the son of the gentleman will care for nothing but riding swiftly, bearing arms, striking with his sword, and wearing finery—each according to his nature. Wherever you may be you will see this every day: that the good man of good stock will show his origin, and that the wretch of base stock and lineage, however high his rank or great his wealth, will never show anything but the baseness of his ancestry. Even though he should dress himself in cloth of gold, or array himself like an emperor, what he wears will always seem to be borrowed, and he will look like an ass at a jousting. Therefore, when such men and women come into power they do not use it as it should be used. As the proverb has it: *The dog donned hunting breeches and no longer recognized his companion.*

Thus, since women are inferior to men, the moment they achieve power and authority, woe to him who is their subject and must obey them! For they have no discretion in commanding or forbidding, but cast aside all good sense and at all times give free rein to their whims and willfulness. Two things are worthy of note: that there never was a woman who was satiated with wealth, nor a drunkard with drinking, for the more he drinks the thirstier he gets. Hence, a wicked woman of evil habits is not only avaricious, but envious, evil-spoken, thieving, gluttonous, undependable in her word, a two-edged sword, disobedient to authority, haughty, vainglorious, a liar, a lover of wine once she has tasted it, a chatterbox and a betrayer of secrets, lecherous, the root of all evil, ready for every wickedness, and fickle in love. I say this only of wicked women, for of good women it is said they have no equal, nor should they be ill-spoken of; rather, they should be placed like a mirror for men to look at.

Hitherto I have spoken of disorderly love and how it should be shunned, and how we should love only God. I will continue now by showing that he who loves trangresses the Ten Commandments and commits all the seven deadly sins, whence all evil arises.

CHAPTER NINETEEN

How he who madly loves trangresses the Ten Commandments

If you desire to know further how dishonest love of man and woman should be despised and condemned, listen carefully to what I shall now tell you: how many evils it gives rise to, how much harm it does to their persons, how many troubles it is the cause of, how many different ways of sinning love is the source of, and how many and how varied are the sins committed because of it. He will be mad who, able to read and understand what I say here, learns not some lesson from it, at least in some degree, even though not entirely.

First I say to you that he who practices, and continues to practice, dishonest love, just to indulge his unbridled appetite, this fellow, I say, transgresses one after the other all the commandments of God. Furthermore, he commits the seven deadly sins, annuls the powers of the spirit, destroys the five senses, corrupts the seven virtues (the four cardinal virtues as well as the three theological ones), and neglects to practice the seven works of mercy. By causing these wicked things mad love brings its practitioners to the pains of hell. This sin, therefore, should be called the root of all evil, since it causes and brings about such great harm, and so many ills follow from it.

CHAPTER TWENTY

How he who madly loves breaks the First Commandment

The First Commandment is: *Thou shalt love thy God above all things.* I ask you now whether he who dishonestly loves the wife, or the daughter, or the kinswoman of his neighbor, to dishonor her, whether this fellow really loves God. It would seem not. Rather, he withdraws from Him and says: "Lord, it is true that Thou didst command me to love none but Thee who art my Lord and Creator; but, Lord, please forgive me if I love this woman more than Thee, for I well know, O Lord, that Thou art so merciful that, although I sin against Thee in this, Thou wilt forgive me. I shall confess and repent, and shall be forgiven at once by Thee."

Thus in the hope of pardon you do wickedly, and even before you commit your sin you have thought how you will deceive God again and again. This comes from His great patience and from His desire for your repentance. And thus you offend God continually and fail to mend your way. Therefore I say unto you that you are taking bad advice, for the love of God is founded upon virtue, and the love of a man for a woman, or that of a woman for a man, is founded upon sin. What is worse, you err in the hope of forgiveness, and that is the origin of all our trouble. In this we need God's mercy, and very much do we need it! Know, then, that he who loves another more than God scorns his Creator and places the creature above Him; he casts virtue aside and loves sin, and, moreover, trespasses against His First Commandment.

CHAPTER TWENTY-ONE

Of the Second Commandment

He who madly loves also transgresses the Second Commandment which is: *Thou shalt not take the name of the Lord in vain.* I ask you, for God's sake, who is there who walks and lives with mad love who does not swear and take the name of God in vain, not once, but an infinite number of times and in a thousand different ways? For he says: "I swear by God and St. Mary and all the Holy Gospels, and even by the saints in Paradise that I'll do thus and so for you. Do not doubt it, for you know I am a Christian. And if that isn't the truth, then I'm a liar! On my conscience, lady, if you will do what I ask I'll give you stuffs and jewels; I'll give you florins and doubloons; I'll make you queen; I'll have all your kinfolk and neighbors coming to gape at you." And so on, according to the greater or smaller estates of the lovers and their persons.

The rascal knows, of course, that he will go back

on his word and give her nothing, but will mock her and fill her ears with wind. And she who believes a man who swears in this fashion will be blinded with tears. Lovers then commit another error even worse and they do not conceal it, that is, they believe they are not obligated to honor or fulfill the vows they swear to their mistresses. Woe to the filthy mouth by which the Creator of heaven and earth, and of the perjurer himself, is so audaciously called upon to attest its lies! A curse on him who thus shamelessly brings as witness to his perjury Him who is truth itself, even Jesus Christ, for the purpose of lying and deceiving his neighbor! There have been, and are, indeed, some who have sworn to marry certain women, and women who have sworn to marry them, either before witnesses or in secret, merely to deceive one another. God help us! An infinity of these vows are broken in subtle ways, for they were only meant to deceive. Upon my word, I say that such wretches do deceive, but that they deceive themselves more than others.

Not to be prolix I will speak no further of this false swearing, for ten quires of paper would not suffice to exhaust the subject. In this as in the other commandments I will be brief and to the point, for to attempt to tell everything would be a long affair, and, anyway, each man can consider it more or less in the light of his own experience. To bring the discussion of this commandment to a close, then, it is evident that he who madly loves does not love God, thus violating the First Commandment, and that he takes His Holy Name in vain—worse, not only in vain, but swears falsely, thus violating the Second Commandment, and so we have two commandments transgressed by him who madly loves.

CHAPTER TWENTY-TWO

⌐ *Of the Third Commandment*

The Third Commandment is: *Thou shalt keep the Sabbath Day and the holy feast days ordained by the Universal Church.* Well now, tell me, you lover, what sabbaths and holy days have you not broken in your mad career, neglecting to go to Mass or prayers, as is your obligation, so that God will have mercy on you? Have you not, on some sabbath or holy day, taken just a few steps to see her whom you most love? Knight or squire, have you not taken part in joustings, tourneys, or other deeds of arms, on Christmas or Easter, or on days dedicated to rest and prayer and the praise of God? Have you not, instead of serving God, ridden beyond the city or village where you dwell to see the one you love? Have you not attended weddings, frolics, and parties to see your mistress instead of serving God and visiting the poor and needy? Have you not traveled leagues on forbidden days, as I have said, to see your mistress and do other things too many to describe? Tell me, then, whether or not you have broken this commandment in your mad love. You have indeed, no doubt about it!

Who is the lover who would not do the same, in whole or in part? For it is a safe rule, as experience proves, that no lover will transgress the commandment of his wretched mistress for anything in the world, or fail to take the greatest pains not to transgress it, for he well knows that his instant reward will be a sour face, a hair-pulling, or a slap. So, fearing to disobey her, he groans and has recourse to every kind of flattery and sweet talk and address, to do whatever she commands, in whatever place, at whatever hour, day, month, or year, for he may not be absent a single moment. The commandment of God, on the other hand, he puts off and stretches like a wet skin, falsifying it, shrinking it, scorning it, and doing with it what he would not dare to do with the command of an equal. This he can do because of the great generosity and infinite goodness and mercy of Him who is always quick to pardon; but justice will be served in the end. We may conclude, therefore, that he who madly loves, in his loving violates the days of rest ordained by God and dedicated to His service, which is the Third Commandment.

CHAPTER TWENTY-THREE

↱ *Of the Fourth Commandment*

The Fourth Commandment is: *Honor thy father and thy mother and thou shalt live long in this world.* Tell me now, have you never transgressed this commandment, when your father or your mother told you or counseled you: "Son, for the love of God give up the love of such and such a woman, for she is very dangerous and it may do you harm"? They did not counsel you thus for zeal or for the love of God, but rather from fear of losing you, lest some night or day the friends and kinsmen of your mistress should seize and kill you, or lest she in jealousy of another woman poison or bewitch you, which are things that happen regularly these days. Tell me, how patient were you in answering them? Tell me, what honor did you show them? Tell me, above all, whether on that occasion you did not get stubborn, answering them with harsh and angry words, honoring neither him who begot you nor her who conceived, bore, and nursed you, adding to this the many other kinds of insults that parents receive from their sons for advising them not to love madly and ruin themselves?

God help us! There are some accursed sons, deserving to be swallowed up by the earth, who for this reason wound their father or mother, or strike them with their fists, or push them about arrogantly. You do the same with your aged godparents who are responsible for you, and with other old people who in honor may be called your parents, and who, when they see you going astray, advise you in kindness and charity to take care of yourself. And you haughtily reply: "My friends, do you know what's good for you? Look after yourselves, for I know what side my bread is buttered on. *A madman knows more in his own house than a sane man in his neighbor's.* Don't bother me. I've been weaned." Etc.

See then how mad love breaks this commandment, for a lover gives it no more importance than if it were issued by some person of the town. And see how he who loves transgresses the Fourth Commandment, dishonoring his father and mother, bringing evil upon them and showing them little respect.

CHAPTER TWENTY-FOUR

↱ *Of the Fifth Commandment*

The Fifth Commandment is: *Thou shalt not kill.* Tell me now, have you never seen, heard, or known of a man who loved some woman, or of a woman who loved some man, who killed for this reason? I say that those killed, or caused to be killed, on this account are numberless. For one thing, a lover will kill a man who has made known his affair, or has insulted his mistress in public or secretly, or has tried to seduce her, or because of any one of the ten kinds of jealousy, which I shall not describe, lest I be prolix and a teacher of evil. And have you never seen or heard of a woman who killed her husband, brother, cousin, or some other kinsman, just to have her will with her lover? And have you never seen a mother consent to the murder of a son or daughter in order not to be discovered, because the said son or daughter had learned or heard of her sin?

In Tortosa I saw a woman executed who had got her lover to murder her son to prevent her exposure. I saw her burned with my own eyes! All this because her son had said to her: "I'm going to tell my father that you have slept with Irazón the painter." So the mother told her lover about it, and between them they decided that the lad, who was only ten, should die. And the lover killed him, and he and the mother buried him in a stable. A pig dug the body up later and so the affair was discovered.

And have you never seen a lover who, to get money so that he could run off with his mistress, killed his father and robbed him? I saw a woman called La Argentera arrested in Barcelona who strangled her father and brought her lover to the house, and they robbed him, and the next day they said he had suffocated with a quinsy. Later I saw her hanged for her crime, and she was one of the most beautiful women of that city. The story of her execution would be too long to tell, but the last episode of it was that the hangman, after he had cut her down, lay with her. So he was condemned to be hanged himself, but through the intervention of friends he was let off with a whipping through the streets of Barcelona. This happened in the year twenty-eight. There should be a lesson even in this for those who defy God and His justice, for the woman was kept in jail for a long time for this crime, although so many pleaded for her that the authorities were inclined to release her. I talked with her in jail myself and spoke for her and got others to do so, but she refused to leave unless acquitted. Meanwhile her lover was caught and put to the torture; confessed, but escaped. So she was hanged, and it was the judgment of God that she should bear the guilt for the murder of her father. It was God's will also that she might live and do penance, but she would not have it so, and thus she died. And even after her death she was the occasion for the hangman's dishonor, because, alas! there are people who in life or death always do evil, or are the cause of every evil, for they were born under that sign.

In the said city of Tortosa I saw with my own eyes two things very hard to believe, but, by God, I saw them! A woman cut off the privy parts of a lover of hers, a man named Juan Orenga, a native of Tortosa and an etcher of swords, because she learned that he was sleeping with another woman. I went to see him and he told me how she had tricked him. It was like this: she had complained to her husband that she could not protect herself from the young man. Her husband was the master of a ship that carried wheat and wool, but he dared not do what his wife asked, because her lover had many kinsmen in the city. So he said: "Wife, I'll load my ship for Barcelona, and while I'm at sea do whatever you think best." The woman went at once on a Monday morning to see her lover, who was setting up his tent and hanging his swords in a showcase. And she said to him: "Orenga, my husband left town this morning. You may come whenever you like." He heard her with pleasure, and she went home and got a razor and hid it carefully under the mattress. She also arranged the bolts on the staircase and the street door so that she could lock them after her when she fled. The lover arrived, armed with his sword and buckler, and she said to him: "Put by your arms, for well I know that you are not going to need them." And he trusted her and did so. And he began to frolic with her and tried to lay her on the bed, but she would not consent, wishing to stay near the place where she had the razor hidden. So he, half exhausted, had to do as she wished, but by this time he was so cold that he was unable to act. When she saw how things were she took his privy parts in her hand, laughing, and playing with them, and when she saw that the time was ripe, she reached under the mattress and got her razor and cut them off entirely, even gashing his thigh a bit, and she said to him: "You traitor! These will never again be of any use to you, or to me or anyone else!" Then she ran down the stairs and bolted the door after her, while he lay there bleeding to death, and in that condition he was taken away.

I witnessed another case, in which a wife bit off her husband's tongue. This she did by getting him in jest to put his tongue in her mouth, and she closed her teeth and cut it off, and he was left dumb and mutilated. The wife then fled to a Franciscan nunnery, where she was arrested for her crime. She said she had seen her husband talking often and secretly with a woman she suspected, and she had said to him: "You will never speak to her again, or deceive another!"

I could tell you of many other murders and mutilations like these, but nowadays such goings-on are so common that it would be superfluous to go into them. Hence it follows that he who loves violates the Fifth Commandment, murdering or consenting to murder.

CHAPTER TWENTY-FIVE

↱ *Of the Sixth Commandment*

The Sixth Commandment is: *Thou shalt not steal.* Tell me now, have you never stolen in order to regale your mistress? And if by chance you had nothing to give her and you knew that she loved you only for what she could get out of you, well then, did you not steal or pilfer from God and His saints to regale and please her? I think you did! And, if you deny it, tell me then, have you never stolen jewels, money, and other things in order to be welcomed when you went to see her? Have you never stolen from your father or your mother for your mistress? Or stolen bread, wine, meat, and other things from your master in order to regale and support her whom you loved and desired? Or, if you have a wife, have you never stolen her jewels, clothing, and a few other things, such as rings, caps, hair nets, veils, wimples, earrings, bracelets, and the like, to give your mistress? Such thefts, however well concealed, are the source of much harm and many scandals and evils, when they are discovered. And have you never stolen fruit, green and ripe, and roses and other things from your neighbor's vineyard and garden to give your mistress, destroying what he has planted and cultivated? Have you never stolen pears, apples, melons, sweet lemons, oranges, and limes for your ladylove? The lover cannot help being a thief, for he would steal from the foot of the Cross to regale his mistress. See, then, how dishonest love causes the lover to steal in order to satisfy his mistress, and thus to break the Sixth Commandment. Would that I might describe the infinite kinds of thievery, too many to count!

CHAPTER TWENTY-SIX

⌐ *Of the Seventh Commandment*

The Seventh Commandment is: *Thou shalt not commit fornication or lechery*. It would be idle to dwell upon this commandment, since it is true and notorious that lovers violate it to satisfy their unbridled will and appetite, although it does happen at times that some of them love truly and wish to marry their mistresses, or take them for companions, sensing good habits and honest virtues in them, while others wish to marry them for their beauty and grace. But for every one of such lovers there are a hundred who mock and betray them. This is the reason for all their parties, balls, and dances, all their merrymaking, their singing and playing, all their love letters and joustings and tourneys and bullfights, their feasts, their fine clothes and better boots, and the rest—all of which has the single purpose of winning those they love best, merely to betray them. Moreover, once they have succeeded, how many dishonest acts of lechery they commit, not to be mentioned here or described! Therefore, although they think they are committing only one mortal sin, because of it they commit many others in their mad career. Let him who will, therefore, consider that the greater his delight in sin, the greater will be his punishment and retribution. So, my son, drink your fill, for you will pay the bill! Your pain will come when it is presented. Your sin is committed in song and laughter, but is purged and paid for in sadness and tears. This, then, is what unbridled love does: in lechery it violates the seventh of God's commandments.

CHAPTER TWENTY-SEVEN

Of the Eighth Commandment

The Eighth Commandment is: *Thou shalt not bear false witness*. I ask you whether you have never borne false witness against man or woman for love of your mistress? If you deny it I will prove it to you. Tell me, how many times have you been asked: "My friend, what kind of woman is So-and-so?" And you answered: "She is a false and wicked woman of vicious habits, open to the first one who comes along; a chatterbox, a drunkard, and a liar; filthy, treacherous, and vile." And you said this perhaps because she would not arrange to have you meet or speak with the one you loved, or because she was her neighbor and said something about you, that she had seen you come and speak with your mistress, or send servants and letters to her. So you from spite lied about her. Tell me also, have you never, while talking with your mistress, in order to puff her up with pride, told her how genteel she was and defamed some other woman, saying: "What's-her-name is this and So-and-so is that; the first is Pedro's mistress, the second bore a child to Juan; the first sleeps with Rodrigo, the other I saw kissing Domingo"? These and many other things lovers are in the habit of telling their mistresses while they are with them, to show them that they are not the only ones living in sin, since there are many others in town—this to comfort the silly fools so that they will not consider themselves fallen because they love and commit this sin, for misery loves company. So the lover bears false witness against women who he knows are quite innocent of his charges. This, then, is what unbridled love does in many ways: it causes lovers to bear false witness, which is to transgress the Eighth Commandment.

CHAPTER TWENTY-EIGHT

⌐ Of the Ninth Commandment

The Ninth Commandment is: *Thou shalt honor thy neighbor's wife as thine own.* It is superfluous to speak of this commandment, for you have already seen how lovers honor their neighbors' wives! Let God protect them who can, and let the neighbor beware of having a beautiful wife! Otherwise, he who seems to be his best friend will be the very one who will set about betraying him. At times the poor fool, moved by good feeling and brotherly love, will invite or bring his friend to his house and make him welcome, and the traitor will cast his eyes upon the wife and think how he can win her away from him. As the proverb has it: *A man sometimes brings to his house the cause of his grief.* The base and good-for-nothing characters who do such things should be called out. On the other hand, all friends are not alike in this, for there are good ones as well as bad. At the same time it is a questionable thing to bring a young friend to your house if you have a young wife. I will say nothing further, but rest my argument on the proverb that says: *Fire next to tow is a dangerous thing.* At times it is the wife who is at fault, at times it is the husband who consents to it, at times the friend who desires it, for there are men who will not keep their hands off a woman, regardless of friendship or kinship. And if a man will not respect his kinswoman, what will he do with the wife of his friend?

Let every married man, therefore, or unmarried, for that matter, if he is halt or one-eyed or ugly, since it is such who commonly have beautiful wives, beware of bringing to his house a well set up, robust, and good-looking young man, for he should know that his wife's eye will wander in that direction because of the desire that women have of knowing men of fashion and presence who understand the ways of the world. This they do because they see themselves fair and wasted on stupid, filthy, and worthless husbands, covered with blemishes, deserving to play the bagpipe. (Of friars and abbots I will say nothing, for they are beasts of prey who, having nothing of their own, steal from their neighbors.) Nowadays men do not speak of their wives in this connection, for it is a shameful thing for them and shows a lack of constancy in their wives if they say: "Don't bring that man to the house, for if you do there'll be a scandal." Or else, when they see a man leave a house where there is a handsome wife, they at once jump to conclusions and say: "It's too bad for the poor devil who's out working, for What's-his-name has just been frolicking in his house!" They say the same of others of higher station: "The squire is off at the frontier and there is So-and-so putting horns on him!" They do not say: "To be sure I know that So-and-so frequents her house, but she enjoys such a good name for chastity that she would not consent, however much he may desire it." But they talk as if all they have to do is to enter, demand, and collect. I say, therefore, that they pay no attention to the fact that such women will refuse and resist them for their honor's sake, for once a man is in the house the fat is in the fire. He will talk and that is the end of it, for he has no regard for her and says that women yield as soon as asked. Consider well, therefore, as I have said above, how little the wife of a neighbor is respected these days by his friends or by strangers. Hence we may say that the Ninth Commandment is broken and transgressed because of mad love, in disorderly covetousness, common and general among all men.

CHAPTER TWENTY-NINE

Of the Tenth Commandment

The Tenth Commandment is: *Thou shalt not covet.* Here it is hardly necessary to say anything, for daily experience teaches us how often lovers in their willful desire covet their neighbors' daughters, wives, nieces, and sisters, or any women who may belong to others, not with good intentions or proper love, but with unbridled covetousness, to sin with them and satisfy their disorderly appetite. And to this rule I make no exception, either for emperors, counts, dukes, or other lords, for once they cast their eyes upon a beautiful woman they covet her forthwith and use their power to possess her. But, as for their own wives and kinswomen, these must be guarded and let no one fall in love with *them*, and let him who does so die, although they give the serving maids of their own households no rest! They, however, must be as free as Tamburlane's camel, which could graze where it listed, with no hindrance whatever. Thus, they are very jealous in guarding their own, but free to spoil what belongs to another and to dishonor their own kin.

Consider briefly, therefore, how disorderly love brings about the violation of all the Ten Commandments ordained by God. Who is so blind or mad that he will, for a moment of vain and foolish love, cause so much harm? So we may well conclude that mad love is the source of all evil; further, that love is the cause of our committing the seven deadly sins, for there is not a single one which is not committed by lovers, as you will see below.

CHAPTER THIRTY

⌐ *Of the first deadly sin*

The first deadly sin is pride, for it is said that a man should not be proud, but patient and humble. According to the *Moralia* of St. Gregory, there are four kinds of pride, namely: first, when a fool thinks that what he possesses he got by his own cleverness and cunning; second, when he thinks that he got it by his own merit; third, when he boasts of possessing what he does not possess; fourth, when he despises others and sets himself up as unique in his ways and deeds. Read the Master of the Sentences, Book II, in the chapter on Pride, and there you will find what I have said, that is, that lovers are more guilty of this sin than others, because they wish to keep up their show of gallantry.

Tell me now, and God save you, have you ever seen a lover who was not haughty, proud, and boastful, so much so that no one must bespeak him without permission, holding all others in scorn, as if they were nothing and the sons of no one, save him alone? His speech high-sounding and pompous, accompanied with grimaces and gestures, and he rising on his toes and stretching out his neck, lifting his eyebrows with eloquence and arrogance, scowling when he hears or sees something not to his taste, very ready in threats to kill and cut throats, so that none dares stand before him? And when he mounts his horse (if his rank be such) and rides through the streets, sparing neither donkey nor ass, or the poor and ill-clad, but bumping them all most rudely without pity or compassion, with the pride and fancy that he has from his lady's love? Very erect in the saddle, his legs stuck out, his feet withdrawn from the stirrups, and he glancing down at them ever and anon, if by chance he is wearing his high boots, and these well greased, his hand on his hip, on his head a great Italian biretta, or a hat like a crown, taking up the whole street with his trotting nag, hack, or mule, striking with his spurs, legs, or feet all those he meets and knocking them about, and shouting: "Out of the way, there! Long live my lovely mistress!"

Who can face this fellow? Who, however bold, can oppose what he says or does, whether it be good or bad, without being eaten alive by the proud young blade? It is the same when he is afoot and armed with sword and buckler. Out of the way, varlets! Here comes the mad lover! Hercules the strong, Goliath the giant, Samson, Alexander, or Nimrod the stubborn could not, he thinks, stand against him. And in the whole neighborhood of his ladylove no man or woman dares to speak to her or gaze upon her, but at once he bursts forth with threats, curses, and prideful boastings. I say the same of nobles, burghers, and other persons, of whatever degree or estate, who madly love, for such is their pride that the world is too small for them, sometimes alone, sometimes under the protection of those they live with. And they strut about with such effect that often they bring about the ruin of the wives and daughters of good men, for, when these women refuse to do their will, then you should hear the gossip, see the libelous lampoons tacked to their doors, and hear the insults shouted at night before their houses! And the women dare not reply or say a word, until eventually they must do willy-nilly what these men would have them do—all this from their pride and power, without fear of God or justice, or shame of the people. You see, then, the first deadly sin here committed, and I could say a great deal more about it, but shall refrain lest I bore you with my longwindedness.

CHAPTER THIRTY-ONE

↱ *Of the second deadly sin*

The second deadly sin is avarice, and who can doubt that they who love in an evil hour fall into it? They are not content with what they have; all the wealth in the world, indeed, would not be enough to pay for their joustings and carryings-on, mad and all decked out. You will never see such open their hands except to give presents to their mistresses, or to those who arrange their affairs, or to those who know about them, or to the pimps and go-betweens of their ladyloves. In this they really let themselves go and never check themselves in giving jewels and stuffs, in eating and drinking and carousing. In all other situations, however, their avarice and stinginess is notorious, for they think, like the toad, that the whole earth is hardly big enough to satisfy their appetite, and they go about seeking those who possess the wherewithal, or can get it for them. But try to take from them a single hair and you will see what I am talking about, unless you happen to be a party to their affairs, for this is the only way to get anything whatever out of them, because they are not in the habit of giving otherwise. Thus you see how the second deadly sin is here committed by those who madly love.

CHAPTER THIRTY-TWO

↱ *Of the third deadly sin*

The third deadly sin is lechery. Well, since everything else derives from and depends upon this sin, and all finely spun kinds of loving are practiced in it, as well as deceits, false promises and oaths, as I explained above when I discussed the Ten Commandments, it follows that every sin must be charged to lechery and the satisfaction of vain appetites. It is manifest, therefore, that he who madly loves falls into the sin of lechery which, doubt it not, he will commit in his mind even if he avoids the act itself. So he is caught in either case, for a sin consented to is called a deadly sin and is counted among their number.

CHAPTER THIRTY-THREE

Of the fourth deadly sin

The fourth deadly sin is envy. Tell me now, what man or woman can be more envious than one who loves? There can be no doubt at all that a lover is envious of his mistress, for he will not allow another to approach her. He is envious of another woman if she is better-looking than his, or has a better figure, or is richer, or of a higher station. He is worried to death about everything and is so envious of other women that he suffers tortures and his liver burns within him. He is envious of lovers who have more comely mistresses. If he is ugly, he is envious of men who are handsome; envious, if he is a cripple, of those who are not; envious, if he is old, of those who are young; envious of those who are wittier, or sing better, or perform better than he any of the infinite things necessary in loving. He is envious if his ladylove casts her eyes upon another whose looks she likes better; envious, if she praises or speaks well of another, and so he says to her: "Well, if you like him so much why don't you run along with him? Or do you want me to bring him to you? You'll have a fine time with him, since you think he's so good-looking!" He is envious if another loves his mistress, and this really hurts! He is envious of others who are more skilled in loving, or do nobler deeds, or are richer and more powerful, or have better figures; envious, to get and possess, as he will, ornaments and fine clothes and jewels, so that he may make a brave show in the game of *cañas*.[2] And what I say of these fellows applies equally to all those I have mentioned before. You see, therefore, how he who loves cannot avoid the sin of envy.

CHAPTER THIRTY-FOUR

⌐ *Of the fifth deadly sin*

The fifth deadly sin is gluttony. He who loves women, or is loved by them, cannot avoid eating and drinking to excess with his mistress, at breakfasts and suppers and dinner parties. There is no end to his buying of capons, partridges, chickens, kids, geese, mutton (or beef if he is a farmer), white wine and red (let water run to the river!) and fruits of many kinds, no matter where they come from or how much they cost. In the spring, *borrincos*,[3] cherries, plums, apricots, peaches, early figs, melons, russet pears from La Vera, crabapples, safflower, sweet and bittersweet pomegranates, red figs, and muscat grapes; in winter, rashers of bacon baked in wine and garnished with sugar, sausages spiced with ginger and cloves, shortbread encrusted with sugar, partridges cooked in sweet wine, and good mulled wine for breakfast. Have a good time! You scratch my back and I'll scratch yours! Life is short, so away we go!

So you see how all this business turns your senses topsy-turvy, destroys your will power, unseats your reason, and muddles your understanding. But have your fun, your frolics and feasting, and weep about it afterward! In the evenings it's sugar candy, lemonade, boxes of sweetmeats, coriander, anise, jellies, and pine nut paste, honey water and sugar cakes, and many other kinds of precious dishes that spur the appetite for eating and drinking, more than is lawful. Then it's rose water and orange blossom water perfumed with musk, in great abundance, and Sevillian or Catalan perfumers filled with benzoin, storax, flax, aloes, laudanum, and willow charcoal made into little lamps for burning. And then it's collations, suppers, breakfasts, and luncheons, in which you cannot avoid eating and drinking to excess. It follows, therefore, that excessive eating and drinking of many and diverse precious things are the cause of lechery, and that disorderly love is the cause of it all. You see, then, how he who loves, loving, commits the sin of gluttony.

CHAPTER THIRTY-FIVE

⌐ *Of the sixth deadly sin*

The sixth deadly sin is anger. As I have already said when I discussed the sin of pride, there is nothing more wrathful than a lover or his mistress if you suggest anything that does not lead to their good or

pleasure. At such a moment the anger of a lover
is so great that it cannot be contained, especially if
his mistress has not responded to his advances, or
he becomes so morose that if he can get some unlucky man or woman into a dispute, he will most
likely bury them under the sod. Others with their
rages spoil the appetites of their families. Others,
from anger and melancholy, slash at the dogs and
animals they happen to pass. Still others shatter
their swords on the stones from pure rage, and bite
their cheeks and lips, grind their teeth, and shoot
fire from their eyes. Or they beat and abuse their
mules and horses; or they neglect to feed them until
night; or they strike them over the head with the
peck measure—all this from rage and ill temper,
because their mistress did not yield to them or
looked crossly at them, and they say: "Damn the
whore and daughter of a whore! She gave me the
eye, she winked at me, she did this and that, and
now she throws me over! She says 'Come here' with
her eyes and holds me off with her hands. By God's
body, the devil must have got me into this mess!"
Meanwhile, they get so furious that they almost
burst, and they say: "Damn and blast me for an
unbeliever! By the Body and the saints, I met this
woman in an unlucky hour! When I have presents
for her she's all smiles; when I haven't, she turns
her back!" So it is that lovers are visited with anger
in many ways, too many to be recounted here. Thus
you see how you commit the sixth deadly sin by
loving and being loved.

CHAPTER THIRTY-SIX

↱ *Of the seventh deadly sin*

The seventh deadly sin is sloth, and it is well committed by him who loves, for he is diligent only in those things that concern his love. In all else he is lazy, slow, and sleepy. You could not move him, even with a lever, to do a good deed. He is dilatory in his own affairs and untrustworthy in his neighbor's, so much so that let no man ask him to work save at his love. In it he puts all diligence, all heart, all will. Tell me now whether it is not slothful to lie abed with your mistress until high noon, and even to eat and drink with her in bed! Tell me whether it is not pure laziness when, the lover being in bed, he is told: "Get up now, for you have such and such an affair to attend to." And he, yawning and stretching, replies: "Go away! There's time enough for that later on." Or when he is told: "Sir, or friend, look, you have been called to a council meeting, or to take care of this or that piece of business." Or "You, priest, have been called to say early Mass, or matins, or vespers." This according to the station of each. And he answers: "I can't come now; I'm ill." Or "I didn't sleep last night." Or "Tell them you couldn't find me." Or "Tell them I'm not at home." Or "Tell them I'll be along later." All this because of his great sloth, or because he will not leave his dear rib. Or he says he is sweating and would catch cold if he got up. See, then, how he who madly loves commits the seventh deadly sin.

And now if we ask ourselves what men are apt for loving, what qualities they must have, and how they

must act in order to be successful, here we shall discover what kind of people lovers are, and whether
or not they disgrace themselves with their noisiness,
their playing and singing in the streets and squares,
and shouting for all the world to hear: "Look at
me! I'm in love with What's-her-name and I want
you to know it!" As if they were reading a royal
edict! Such are the town criers, the instruments,
lutes, guitars, harps, and bandurrias; such the rebecs,
fiddles, and tambourines; such the trumpets! On the
other hand, although it is true that each of them
says he loves, very few are really equipped for loving, nor are their mistresses for being loved. In a
word, he who is stricken with mad love transgresses
all the Ten Commandments, as you have heard, or
the greater part of them, and he practices and commits most of the deadly sins.

Consider, therefore, my friend, how little profit
there is in madly loving and how many evils arise
from it. Let him who is not daft and has a little
sense heed what applies to him; let him know good
from evil and practice what is best and most profitable for him. And he who has ears to hear, let him
listen and put it to good use, for I could hold forth
at great length in the matter of priests, friars, and
nuns in this particular; but in so doing I should be
speaking with a single mouth and listening to a
thousand. It would make enemies for me in both
sexes, bring down curses and insults upon me while
I live, and give me a bad time when I am dead. Not
on this account, however, should a man neglect to
tell the truth; but he who reprehends should have
nothing reprehensible in him, and so, since I am not
guiltless myself, it will be prudent for me to speak

little and modestly. In general, it is given to everyone to speak, correct, and teach, but few are well received. As the proverb has it: *Let him who desires to live do as others do; if he doesn't he'll find himself alone and penniless.* I shall cease here, so as not to be prolix and wearisome, for, although in my day I have seen and heard many preachers and others tell the naked truth to kings and nobles, I have also seen them get into plenty of trouble and get silenced, however learned and pious they may have been. He who learns by another's experience is worthy of praise.

CHAPTER THIRTY-SEVEN

How he who loves loses all the virtues

Those who will consider carefully the foregoing arguments will find in them much food for thought, not only those I referred to who transgress the Ten Commandments by giving themselves up to mad love, but those who commit the seven deadly sins and destroy their five senses, or, at any rate, so weaken them that they hardly function as they should, disturbed as they are by mad thoughts. I say, moreover, that the act of lechery deprives a man of his natural judgment and saps his strength, and that gradually day by day he decays until death overtakes him, because he no longer has the power to resist this sin. So let him be called constant and strong who resists its first stirrings. Such strength comes from without and is called fortitude, and constant and strong is he who has this virtue. We may say, therefore, that he who loves lacks fortitude in one way or another, either because he lacks strength, or lacks spiritual and temporal constancy. Temperance, of course, is not to be looked for in him, for he who is not by nature temperate, how can he practice temperance? How, indeed, since temperance is called the middle virtue between two vicious extremes? And justice? Seek it not in him who has it not and cannot practice it, for how can he be just who attempts to seduce, and in fact does seduce, the daughter, wife, or sister of another? Justice consists in giving unto each what is his, and not in depriving one's neighbor of his goods, for he takes his neighbor's goods aplenty who dishonors his wife, daughter, or sister, knowing that afterward she will abandon her father and mother for him—which is legally and properly called stealing, for it is stealing for a man to take another's goods against his will, or usurp them, or swindle him out of them. If he who commits such a crime has any sense, or even if he is mad, let him see, hear, and learn, for that man is called prudent who provides for things before they happen, so as not to be caught unaware when they do. This is a piece of wisdom above all wisdom, so much so that he who is prudent is held to be a diviner, or prophet, or a soothsayer. The fact is that the provident man is called wise and prudent in whom providence is born of, or derived from, prudence, for the provident man is first prudent. Hence, in ancient times prophets were held to be wise men because they foretold the future, sometimes because of their great natural intelligence, but more commonly because the spirit of God was within them.

But, to get back to our argument, he who madly

loves and tries to steal, usurp, take, or dishonor the wife of another, lacks these four virtues, for I certify to you that a father will never give his daughter to you or to anyone else of his own free will; nor a brother his sister; nor a husband his wife. And if you should take her and make a mock of her, know that the other will not like it, however much your lord or bosom friend he may be. If you reply that at times such men give their women to others for money, gifts, or jewels, or that a servant to do his master a great favor, will yield up his sister, cousin, or kinswoman; or a mother her daughter, for gifts or money; or that the vassal will do so for his lord, to reduce his taxes or advance himself; or that any man whatever will do so to gain favor with the great and does not suffer from the dishonor of his sister or kinswoman, then, I say, that unless such a fellow is possessed of the devil, he will never do so willingly, nor will it please him to see those he loves and cherishes in the power of another. Although at first glance it may seem that he is yielding them up willingly, this he does for his interest and not because he wants to. Or it happens at times that he is driven by poverty, for if he has not the means to maintain himself, or to go about in fine clothes, in his madness he yields up his daughter, sister, or kinswoman to one who will provide him with these things.

It sometimes happens that a husband cannot provide his wife with what she needs, and has neither food, drink, nor money for her. And the poor fellow sees that her earnings do not come from her distaff and spinning wheel, or from sewing and embroidering; so he must keep his mouth shut and

put up with it and look the other way, and let his
wife play the cock, while he becomes a hen with
the pip. But woe to him who engages in such commerce, or accepts such payment, or deals in such
goods, or consents, because it would be better, for
the sake of his soul and body, to suffer any evil
rather than consent to evil! Oh, how many gentlemen and those of great estate, laymen as well as
priests, rich and powerful, engage in this commerce
when they hear of a woman or maid who is poor
and beautiful and of poor connections, and with
gifts and money corrupt her in the many subtle
ways they know of, which I shall not describe, lest
I teach evil instead of correcting it! And when they
fail in their purpose they bring quarrels and suits
against her father or mother, or brother, so that
these will send intermediaries to plead with them—
this to achieve their desire with women! Or they
will incite their own kinsmen to quarrel with those
of the woman, to make her come and plead with
him, and the great lord will put on a show of rage,
so that the father, mother, and kinsmen of the girl
will have to accept the charge and do as he desires.

These and other cunning devices are employed by
some in order to have their way with the weak. Woe
to the soul that is guilty of such villainy! And woe
even to the body when after the Judgment body
and soul will be joined again! Whoever considers
this will refrain from such acts, that is, if he considers how the sinner will be called strictly to account, even for his most idle and harmless word.
And, if that is so, what will be the fate of the
wicked who speak evil for the purpose of doing
evil, libeling, defaming, and dishonoring? Would

that I could give you more details, but I say no more. And if this is true of the spoken word, what of the wicked and perverse deeds done for an evil and vengeful purpose? And what of those men who are so wicked in themselves that they can do naught but evil and come to a bad end? They go to the devil and eternal torment, bereft of their judgment and natural understanding, for they neither lead a Christian life nor obey any of the Commandments, nor can they give their power to another to act for them. Woe to the luckless wretch who gives his power to another to order and dispose those things which the other neither knows nor understands! And woe to him who, when he dies, is unable, through cowardice or faintheartedness, or because it was God's will, to dispose of his soul or estate, or order his debts and obligations paid, and gives his power to another who knows little or nothing of it and who will make a will which the dying man never would have made. All the other has to do is to insert in the will a general clause to the effect that *he spoke with the party who told him his wishes and will*—which is a great lie and a flouting of the dead man's wishes.

Cursed be he (and let this be understood by whoever can or will understand) who leaves his last wishes to another, or gives him power to act in his stead! For at the moment of death a man will utter any kind of nonsense, especially since he will be out of his head and unable to say anything but what he is told or ordered to say, or what is put into his mouth, sometimes from fear, sometimes from ignorance or unconsciousness or pain, or because he is dim of understanding. The healthy man looks furiously upon the sick one, threatening that he will kill him when the others have gone, if he does not consent and say "yes." In this and other ways he is forced to say "yes" who if left to himself would say "no," and all because he put it off to the last moment when he could no longer help himself, and became a slave when he could have been master. I wish I could describe all the tricks practiced upon a man in his last hour, but it would be a vexation and a teaching of evil, so my pen ceases.

Know, then, that he is a prudent man who orders his affairs while he is in good health and his right mind, and who disposes of his property with his own hand and entrusts his soul and estate to no one but himself, that is, if he loves his soul more than his body and acts prudently, and I say no more. But I know that if any man should do the contrary he will regret it, for when he dies Our Lord will be his judge, the evil one will be prosecuting attorney, his soul will be the defendant; his advocates the spotless Virgin and the saints and angels of Paradise; the infernal court will be made up of the attorneys of Satan; his soul's defender will be the angel into whose care he was given at birth; the attorney for the prosecution will be the enemy who accuses him; the soul's attorneys will be God, his guardian angel, and his conscience; the witnesses for the dark angel will be the evil works and wicked deeds he did in life; the trial of his soul will concern his life and how he spent his time; the clerk of court will be the world in which he committed his misdeeds; and his sentence will be either great damnation or eternal salvation, where all appeals cease.

So, my friend, beware of what you entrust and to

whom you entrust it, for if any man, fearless of God and His justice, like a blind man does the contrary, regardless of himself and his soul, it will be the effect of his ancient and stubborn perseverance in wickedness, and of the ugly and heavy sins in which he has grown old, for it now seems to him that the killing of men is nothing. It follows as a consequence that in the end Our Lord will be pleased to take his mind away, and because he did not know Him in life, he will not know himself after death, and there will be no memory of him, nor will he be able to confess to Him by his mouth. I ask you, then, whether he is prudent or mad who by madly loving brings upon himself all these evils? He who boasts of such love is devoid of fortitude, even more of temperance; justice does not dwell in him, and prudence is not even visible. For he who has fortitude does not seek to acquire his neighbor's goods by evil devices; he who is temperate does not act outrageously against another; and he who is prudent does not commit such follies. And faith, hope, and charity, seek them not in him, three virtues which with the others make up the seven.

To conclude: we have proved how he who madly loves transgresses the Ten Commandments and commits the seven deadly sins. He fails to practice, besides, the four cardinal virtues; rather, he corrupts them. He destroys the five corporeal senses and diminishes them, for he sees neither the things of this world to do good with them, nor the spiritual; nor can he sense the odors of honesty and modesty, or those of Paradise; nor can he taste the food of the soul or body, to sustain them as he should; nor does he know what he walks upon, or in what world he

lives; nor does he know spiritually how the saints of
Paradise are in glory for the love of God; nor does
he have corporeal or spiritual feeling in his hands,
because they are benumbed by the cold of the great
sin that envelops him. The same is true of his
corporeal and spiritual feet, which are tied, for they
walk neither in pilgrimages nor in good works; nor
do they in contemplation walk through the martyr-
dom of Christ and those who suffered death for
Him. As for works of mercy, when did he ever engage in them? And corporeal works, did he do them
by visiting the sick and heavy-laden? Did he ever
give food and drink to the needy, or redeem cap-
tives, or clothe the poor, or take them up, or protect
them? No, he did not perform even the spiritual
works of mercy, for he was not fit to teach any
good, or to counsel or chastise the erring, or to console them. Neither was he able to suffer insults or to
forgive those offered him, nor can he even support
them. Nor is he able to pray to God and praise Him,
or teach the simple how to rule themselves in order
to live the good life. So, then, he who is guilty of all
this, certain it is that he fails to perform the seven
works of mercy, either spiritual or corporeal.

Therefore, my friend, open your spiritual and
corporeal eyes; look about you and see the many
evils that spring from madly loving, because of
which you will lose not only eternal life, but will
suffer infernal torment. Woe to the wretch who deserves to suffer such cruel and perpetual punishment! Ah, if he would only remember how a little
headache, or ailment, or pain in the side, or in the
hip, or belly, or back, or kidneys, or a fever, either
tertian or quartan, or any other pain or affliction, if

it lasted any time at all, drove him to madness and despair, and how he cursed his fate and the day he was born, or how even a little thorn in his foot or hand or finger made him howl with pain, or a toothache, or an eye ache, or earache, or gout, or sciatica, or a sprained leg or arm or finger, or any one of the thousand ills that people suffer—well, then, how will he be able to stand those other punishments and cruel torments, beyond comparison more painful than those he suffered in life? On earth he had recourse to the remedies of physicians, and herbs and medicines, but in the other world there is no hope or remedy, save for the souls in Purgatory.

Thus much for the soul, but later on, at the Last Judgment and Resurrection, when the soul shall have recovered its body, the body will suffer double the pain it suffered before. Body and soul will suffer together and curse their Creator, and the soul will curse the year, month, day, hour, point, moment, and instant it was created. The body likewise will curse the day it was conceived, engendered, given life, born, and reared, and will curse its father and mother and the milk it sucked, the years it lived in the world, its disordered will and willful appetite, its excessive loving, its lack of sense, its mad and delirious brain. It will curse the ugly sins that brought it to such a pass, and will curse itself for refusing to believe in and know its God and Creator, and its conscience which it would not listen to. Thus, in suffering and torment, like a madman it will damn itself to hell, in the knowledge that its pains will have no end. And living it will die, and dying it will live in new pains, torments, and suffering every day, world without end!

World without end! If a man would only think upon this, ponder it, mourn over it, know it, remember it, have it engraved upon his heart, and keep vigil over it, evil-doing would not be possible for him. If he would bear in mind the pains he suffers in this world, would he do the evil that he does each day? St. Augustine doubts it. Let no one plead, therefore, saying: "I didn't know; I didn't hear; I wasn't warned; I wasn't told about it," because it would be gross ignorance not to know what is notorious to all the world.

This is not a chronicle or romance of chivalry, in which at times white is made black. Know that what I say here is the truth, and it is folly not to accept it, or the greater part of it. And do not think that he who writes this speaks merely from hearsay, for he witnessed much of it, and studied and read about the rest. With the great and wise doctors of old, he believes that what he says is true, as you can discover for yourself any time you like. Reading about such things is profitable, to be sure, and understanding them is a help, but practice and experience are the best teachers of everything. Let him who writes this write without fear, for he seems to see it as he writes. And let him who reads this doubt it not, for if he reads and diligently examines it he will see that it was all written to put him on the true path. The example of the ancients should be a sufficient example for the living, and it is surely good to profit by the experience of others. What one man went through, with many hardships and dangers and suffering, and what he saw in his own person and wrote down on a piece of paper, let this teach others and serve as a lesson against evil-doing, a remedy for wickedness, and a warning against the pitfalls of this world, and serve to protect and defend them from the devil and from women. And if anyone reads what I have said here and puts it into practice, I pray God that his mending will serve to redeem a few of the sins I once committed, as well as those I commit each day, and, after I am dead, win me pardon for this life of pain and torment, amen!

CHAPTER THIRTY-EIGHT

↱ *Conclusion: How all evils proceed from love*

In view, therefore, of the effect of mad love and the great harm it does, let us examine this thing for which we damn ourselves and see what women are like, what they are good for, what attributes they have for loving and being loved, and, finally, what reason has man to love them. Let it be understood, since I shall presently explain some of the vices and evil living of women, that I speak only of those who find it impossible to put away their vices and wicked ways, refining out, as gold from dross, the virtuous, the honest, and the good, for if evil is not reproved, virtue is not praised. By Our Lord God, I verily believe that, just as gold is prized among the metals and shines out above them, so does the honest and wise man or woman shine out like a precious ruby, so much so that comparison is idle. Therefore, I propose to explain and continue with the vices of wicked women which I have mentioned above, showing which are the greater and which the lesser. Let each woman see, therefore, whether she

is the guilty one, and let her scrutinize her conscience closely and not plead her bad luck. She who
takes this to heart will make no mistake. So I will
begin with the sin of avarice in women, but if any
man should find that it applies to him, let him consider it an example of the saying: *I was speaking to
her, but I meant you!* And I do not except myself
from the number of sinners until the day of my
death.

Here ends the first part of my book.

⌐ PART TWO

Here begins the second part of this book which, as I have said, will expose the vices, blemishes, and evil ways of wicked and vicious women, applauding the virtuous in their virtues.

CHAPTER ONE

Of the vices, blemishes, and evil ways of perverse women, and first I shall speak of avarice

Since one cannot write or say the half of what could be said or written of evil, vicious, dishonest, and infamous women, and since telling the truth is not a sin, but a virtue, I shall begin by saying that the greater number of women are born avaricious. It is because of their avarice that many of them commit an infinity of wicked acts, for, if money, precious jewels, and other fineries are offered or given them, beyond a doubt the strongest of them will succumb. It is likely, indeed, that the avaricious woman, whether of great estate or lowly, will commit any wickedness because of her unbridled appetite for possessing.

An example of this happened in Barcelona. A certain queen was very honest, but not without vanity, for she thought she was more virtuous than any woman, and she used to go about saying: "What woman is so base that she would yield her body to a man for all the wealth in the world?" She repeated this so frequently and publicly that a certain nobleman swore by the True Cross that he would persuade her to yield up her body for gifts, or die in the attempt. So he said to her one day: "My lady, what a beautiful ring you have and what a beautiful diamond! Tell me, my lady, if a man should give you another ten times as precious, would you love him?" And she replied: "I would not love him if he gave me one a hundred times as precious!" Then said the nobleman: "My lady, if a lord should give you a ruby that shone like a torch, would you love him, my lady?" And she replied: "Not if it shone like four torches!" But the nobleman persisted and said: "My lady, if a man should give you a city as great as Rome was at its height and make you mistress of the whole world, would you love him, my lady?" And she replied: "Not even if he gave me the kingdom of Castile!"

When the nobleman saw that he was making no headway with gifts he tempted her with power, saying: "My lady, if a man should make you empress of the world so that all the men and women would come to kiss your hands as their sovereign, would you love him?" At this the queen sighed deeply and said: "Oh, my friend, could any man give so much?" Here she fell silent, and the nobleman smiled and said to himself: "If I had something to give her now, I could have this wicked woman in my hands!" And the queen pondered and saw that she had said an evil thing, and she recognized that no steel is strong enough to stand against gifts, to say nothing of a person of flesh and blood, who is naturally subject to unbridled cupidity.

You may take it for granted, therefore, that if gifts can break stones, a woman, who is not as strong as a stone, will yield to them. Why, with gifts you can make the pope himself give you whatever you desire! Item: with gifts you can make emperors, kings, and lesser men obey you. Item: with jewels and gifts you can pervert justice. Item: with gifts you can make truth out of lies. So then, be not astonished if gifts bring about the downfall of honest women and cause them to lose their honor and good name, for a gift respects neither place, station, nor wealth, but twists everything to its purpose. Believe me, therefore, avarice is so strong in woman that you will rarely see her succor the needy. Rather, her single thought is to secrete, like a magpie, what she gets. Thus, a wife will hide things from her husband, a mistress from her lover, sister from brother, cousin from cousin. Moreover, however much they have, they are always crying and complaining of their poverty, and they say: "I haven't got anything; I can't get anything; the people despise me. What is to become of me, poor wretch?" And if they spend something of their own, however little, they first bemoan it a thousand times and complain of it before and after. It happens with them as with the two philosophers, Epicurus and Imprimas,[4] for the god of Epicurus was eating and that of Imprimas was drinking, and they believed there were no other gods, and both ended their days in this belief. Thus, a woman thinks there is no other good in the world but getting, holding, keeping, and possessing, guarding her own with care and spending other people's money generously.

You will learn by experience that a woman will make more noise over spending a farthing than a man over spending a pound. For example, she will scream like mad and poison the ears of her household over the loss of an egg. "What became of my

egg? Who took it? Who stole it? Where is my egg?
Although it was white, it is black and unlucky today! Whore and daughter of a whore, tell me, who
took my egg? Let whoever eats it be eaten by
rabies! Alas, my egg of the double yolk, I was sav-
ing thee for hatching! Alas, my egg! What a cock
and what a hen would have issued from thee! Of the
cock I'd have made a capon worth twenty farthings,
and the hen would have brought fourteen! Or perhaps I should have set her and she would have
hatched out so many cockerels and pullets, and they
would have so multiplied, that they would have got
my feet out of the mud! But now I am luckless and
poor as I was. Alas, my lovely egg of the round
tread and shell so thick! Who has eaten thee?
Marica, you whore, you glutton, you have driven
me out of my house! I swear I'll blister your cheeks
for you, you low, filthy pig! Alas, my egg! What
will become of me now, poor forlorn wretch that I
am! Jesus, my friend, why don't I die and get it over
with? Alas, Virgin Mary, how can one see such a
thing and not burst with rage? Not to be mistress
of a single egg in my own house, poor fool! A
curse on my life! I've a good mind to scratch my
face and tear out all my hair, by God! Woe to her
who brings the bran in the morning and builds a
fire and bursts her cheeks blowing to make it burn,
and, when it's burning, puts on the kettle and heats
the water, and cooks a mash to make her hens lay,
only to have her eggs snatched from her as soon as
laid! Lord, what a tribulation! What a heartache! I
save up my eggs, woe is me, and try to do what God
commands, and the devil steals them from me! Take
me from this world, O Lord, so my body will suffer

no more pain and my soul no more bitterness! By Thy Holy Name, O Lord, give strength to my heart to endure the troubles I face each day! One death would be better than so many, by God!" Thus do women scream and cry about nothing.

In like fashion, if a woman loses a hen she will go from house to house and stir up the whole neighborhood. "Where is my hen, the white one with the red legs?" Or "Where is the one with the double crest, the dark gray one with a neck like a peacock's and purple legs, the good layer? May his days be numbered, he who stole her! May he come down with tumors, pain in the side, and deadly rabies when he eats her! May he never eat another! May his dinner be accursed, amen! Alas, my white hen! Thou gavest me an egg each day. May he who ate thee be cast out of his house! May I see him eaten by dogs, and soon! Alas, my hen, fat as a goose, my Moorish hen with the yellow feet! She was worth any two I have left, woe is me! She was here but a moment ago and flew out the door and over the roof, after the cock. And just the other day, miserable creature that I am, born in an evil hour, poor wretch, I lost my cock, the good crower, the father of as many chicks as there are stars in the sky, who covered my nakedness and succored me in my woes! So long as he was alive my purse was never empty, alas! My Lady of Guadalupe, to thee I commend him! Ah, Lady, forsake me not! Woe is me, only three days ago he was stolen from me! Dear Jesus, how much robbery there is, how much injustice, how much wrong! Hush, friend, in God's name, and let me weep, for I know what I lost then and what I have lost today! Each one mourns for his own, I for such

a jewel as my cock, and now my hen! May a bolt
from heaven and a mortal pestilence strike such
people! When they eat, may a spine or bone get
stuck in their throat, and let not St. Blas help them!
I won't say, my friend, that God is not in His
heaven, but I will say that He is not as he used to
be, since He allows such things to happen and consents to them. O Lord, why dost Thou suffer so
many evils so patiently? By Him who Thou art,
console me in my vexations and heed my anguish!
Otherwise I shall go mad, or kill myself, or turn
Moor! Woe is me, poor wretch, if God will not help
me, for I know not what to say! Leave me, friend,
for a body dies of so much wrong! Even a dog or a
cat will not put up with it! *A wrong a day puts a
strain on courtesy*. Today a hen and yesterday a
cock! Although I am silent, I know where I hurt.
*How did you get bald, my son? Plucking the little
hairs out one by one! How did you get poor, my
lad? Why, losing little by little the little that I had!*
Come here, girls, you daughters of whores! Where
are you? The devil take you! Can't you even say:
'Here, ma'am'? Ha, may you come down with the
plague! Where were you, tell me? It's plain that it
wasn't your hen! Juanilla, run at once to the house
of my gossip and ask her whether she has seen a
white hen with red feet. Marica, go to my neighbor's house and find out whether my white hen
passed that way. Perico, off with you to the archbishop's vicar and get him to give you an excom-
munication, so that the wicked traitor who ate her
will die accursed and unshriven! Juanillo, go call the
town crier and have him cry my hen all over the
neighborhood. Call my cousin Trotaconventos[5] and

tell her to go from house to house looking for my white hen. Damn such a life! Damn such a neighborhood! To think a person can't even own a hen but the moment she goes out the door she is snatched away! Let's go chicken stealing then, for by this mark that God gave me I'll do to all the women who pass my house the same kindness they do to me! Alas, my white hen, and where art thou now?"

These and other things women do for a trifle. They save the chaff and throw away the wheat. They do not stint themselves in buying their long skirts and their dangling sleeves, or the other finery they dishonestly wear, thus ruining their husbands, kinsmen, and lovers, but they put all diligence into acquiring an egg or a hen. And when they trip over their long skirts they say: "The devil take these skirts and the first woman who put them on!" But they do not curse themselves who wear them. And if anyone should cast this up to them they say: "Well, I only do what others do." And they speak truly, for nowadays the wife of a mechanic, even though she has nothing to eat, when she sees the wife of a gentleman all decked out in the latest fashion, will have the same or die trying. They are like monkeys: what they see, that they want. "Did you see What's-her-name last Sunday, how she was got up? Well, burn me if next Sunday I don't wear as good or better!" The clothes that other women wear, the stuff they are made of and its color, their finery, and the gewgaws they carry—all this, I say, is so carefully noted that it is never forgotten. "So-and-so wore this; What's-her-name wore that." Into this kind of thing a woman will put all her heart and

soul, but not into the welfare of her household, her
estate and honor, only into things of vanity and
folly, of little profit. But if her husband is short of
money and is obliged to pawn a coat or cape of hers,
or a ribbon, or some other piece of finery, then you
should hear the sobs, groans, complaints, scoldings,
tears, and curses, and she says: "Unlucky wretch
that I am, I am not so fortunate as my neighbor! Instead of getting richer, I get poorer. Instead of buying me some new clothes, you go and pawn these
poor rags that you gave me for a wedding portion!
Is this the way I expected to prosper with you? Is
this the way the others prosper and get ahead?
Upon my word, I'll never step out of this house,
just to get talked about! I haven't a thing to wear in
public, woe is me! All right, take it all; take whatever's left! Pawn everything! Sell everything! And
then wall me up and never let me go out! That's
what you got it for! Well, I'll give you enough and
to spare! I'll satisfy you! I promise you you'll never
see me go out that door again! I know what I'm
talking about, as God's my witness!" Etc.

Then come the threats, as well you know, for
she will never show you a smiling face or prepare a
good meal, but badly cooked and worse cleaned,
and all this with an abundance of curses. And if the
poor fool of a husband, father, or lover cannot earn
a living, or his business goes badly, or he needs a
little money to support her, and pawns his cloak, his
sword, his armor, his doublet, his boots, and even his
trifles, or sells his house, vineyard, fields, or estate,
she does not scream now; no curses now; no tears or
groans, just so long as her own goods are safe and
her dowry and wedding chest are untouched. Never

mind what happens to the poor fellow's goods, for she will make it up to him with her distaff and spinning wheel. Yes, indeed!

I say the same of women of lofty name and station, some more, some less, and of the great gentlemen, for a few of them have had this experience. And this in women comes from the overwhelming avarice that rules them, and so true is this that there is no woman who is not naturally stingy in giving, liberal in asking and demanding, clever in keeping and holding, reluctant in offering, fearful in lending, large-handed in taking, generous in giving what is not hers to give, ostentatious in dress, boastful in speech, quick to forbid, cruel in commanding, presumptuous in listening, and very hasty in acting.

CHAPTER TWO

How woman is a gossip and a backbiter

That a woman is a gossip and a backbiter may be taken as a general rule, for if she talks with a thousand she talks about a thousand: how they were dressed, the state of their health, how much money they have, their private affairs, their way of living. Silence for her would be death itself. Not for a single hour could she refrain from taking everyone to pieces, good and bad alike. For her there is no such thing as a good man or woman, in the square or at church, but she says: "Oho! And did you see how What's-her-name was got up on Easter Sunday? Why, she was wearing a rich scarlet gown trimmed with marten, a skirt of Florentine silk with strips of marten skin and a six-foot train lined with

brocade, a fur-lined jacket with a collar hanging
down to the middle of her back, brocaded sleeves
with huge knots of gold, twelve to the ounce,
mother-of-pearl bracelets with large beads, gold earrings reaching to her neck, a coif hemmed with
white lilies done in silver, so bright they dazzled
me; in her hair a rich bodkin of fine gold and pearls,
her hair rolled and hung with gold bobs and covered with a linen cap of drawn work edged with
fig leaves, silver sequins, pendants, and little balls,
and trimmed with rich lace. And then, to make her
seem beautiful, she wore a silk kerchief over her
face that made her look like the Queen of Sheba;
arm bands of amber encrusted with gold; on her
fingers ten or a dozen rings, two of diamonds, one
of sapphires, and two of emeralds; gloves trimmed
with marten which she uses to polish her face, with
that toilet water of hers, until it shines like a sword;
a silk handkerchief with gold spangles caught with
a brooch very prettily worked; her pointed slippers
painted and brocaded, with heels a span high, more
or less. Why, she had six servants with her and a
maid to carry her train and a flyflap made of a peacock's tail and perfumed with musk; herself loaded
with civet, even to her eyebrows, and shining like
a sword! Does the flibbertigibbet think she got all
that because she deserved it? But she's the one, she,
who gets herself loved and well loved, and not
I, poor wretch! Why, What's-his-name gave her
everything she's got! She certainly is loved! And
me, I neither love nor get loved, poor fool that I
am! Not all women are born lucky. Take me. Here
I am, ill clad, worse shod, alone and friendless, for
I could never get myself to swindle some man just

so I could have a maid. It's two years now since I
had a new skirt, and I've been wearing this rag for
a year. Haven't I got some reason to complain of
my sad fate, miserable creature that I am, doing
without everything? Why shouldn't I? Am I not
as beautiful as she? And isn't my figure even better?
Is there any reason why I shouldn't be as well
dressed? I haven't lost my beauty on that account,
nor am I less to be gaped at in the square where she
traipses about! With all her finery she's not my
equal! She's a lot of nothing, that's what she is! Bad
luck to the low, filthy, graceless, lazy, misshapen
thing, with her sagging belly, ugly and coarse!
Upon my word, if people only knew what I know
about her they'd blow up at the airs she puts on!
Her teeth are rotten from the white lead she smears
on them, the dirty spider! Her breath stinks like a
dead dog! Take her away, for God's sake! Woe is
me! Here I am, clean as water, neat and well turned
out; working late and earning money, that's what
you will find in me, for a penny in my hand is as
good as a florin in another's. If I were rich, things
would prosper in my hands. What do you say to
that, madam? You can't tell me she isn't getting
paid. She had nothing to begin with, and here after
a month or a year she is rich! But my life is nothing
but a round of work day and night, never getting
ahead. The worst of it is, I'm not known or fa-
vored; on the contrary, I'm looked down upon. My
father wasn't the man *his* father was. God be praised
who loved me so little! It was my bad sign that did
it, because if God had been on earth. . . . I brought
thirty thousand in cash as my wedding portion, and
she came naked to her husband's bed! I'm worse off

than if I were someone's mistress, for I'll never have
any skirt but this thing I'm wearing. May God forgive my father who gave it to me! What have I
got, my friend, since I married you? Why, nothing
but bad luck and spinning day and night! This is
how I spend my life: to bed at twelve, up at three,
hardly any sleep, and eat at noon and then only by
the grace of God! Woe to her who was raised in
her father's house with every luxury and comes
to such a pass! Why and wherefore should this be,
luckless and ill-fated wretch that I am!"

And the mistress says to her lover: "Alack and
woe is me! I'd be better off married, for then I'd be
honored and respected. My downfall dates from the
evil hour when I believed you, poor fool that I was!
This is not what you promised and swore to me!
No sooner do I earn a penny than you snatch it
away from me, saying you're in debt, or that you
gambled, and like a ruffian you kick your hat and
curse it, saying: 'I'm talking to you, hat!' That's
why I've pawned my things and shamed myself
many times, trying to find money to pay your
debts and losses. That's all over now. Where am I
to find money, my friend? God pardon him who
brought me to this pass! There's nothing left for me
now but to be exposed in the stocks with the women
of the town. Woe is me, poor wretch! Others do
better for themselves, but for me, O Lord, a plague
and a fury and a pain in the side!"

This is the way women talk, gossiping and back-
biting and complaining, and they cannot do otherwise. It comes from ancient and stubborn habit and
their ignorance of their own shortcomings, for it is
a terrible sin not to know oneself or one's failings.
So then, in God's name let each man speak of his

neighbor in such wise that he will not offend him.

CHAPTER THREE

⌐⌐ *How women, because of their cupidity, love all comers*

It would be a great sin to doubt that a woman will take and usurp, to right and to left, not only from outsiders and strangers, but from kinsmen and friends, everything she can lay her hands on, and this without fear or shame. Giving is not in her nature. It is like what happens with a husband and wife, or with parents and their son. Let the mother and father give their son everything he wants and never refuse him, and then let them try to get from him a bit of bread or something like that, and he will scream to get it back. Or let the father say to him, merely to test him: "Son, give me this, for I am your father." And the son will run off with whatever it is and hide his face. So it is with a woman: give her something and she will take it singing, but ask for it back and she will burst into tears and scolding. What she gets she hides away in chests and boxes, or ties it up in rags, so that she looks like an old clothes vendor or haberdasher. And when she empties her chest, here you will find mother-of-pearl, there rings, here earrings, there bracelets, many wimples lined with silk, scarves, flounces, three or four linen kerchiefs,[6] richly embroidered cambrics, Catalan toques, headdresses covered with silver work, embroidered arm bands, hair nets, bodkins and other ornaments, coifs, gir-dles, trains, mother-of-pearl bracelets strung with black beads, others of turquoise of various designs, ten thousand stones in each, silk neckcloths, or linen, delicately embroidered or crocheted, sleeves of voile, embroidered blouses (these really matchless), sleeves with cuffs, gathered or ungathered, others embroidered or plain, handkerchiefs by the dozen, not to mention the purses and gold and silver belts, richly worked, pins, a mirror, a powder box, a comb, a sponge and mucilage for laying hair, an ivory bodkin, a pair of silver tweezers for plucking out the little hairs when they appear, a magnifying mirror for making up her face, and a rag for cleaning it with spittle.

Besides all this, she collects ointments, and flasks and pots and cruets where she keeps waters for her face, some to shrink the skin, filtered water to make it shine, and deer, cow, or sheep marrow, which stinks not worse than the devil! She makes soap with the fat of deer kidneys, filtering the water through raw hemp and willow ash, and when the fat is rendered and the fire is burning, she throws the fat into the kettle while the sun is shining very hot, and stirs it for nine days, one hour a day, until the mixture congeals and turns into what they call Neapolitan soap. Then she stirs into it musk and civet, cloves soaked for two days in orange blossom water, or she mixes orange blossom water into it, and this is what she uses for anointing her hands and making them soft as silk. She also has filtered water for tightening the skin of her breasts and hands when wrinkles appear. For the same purpose she makes an emulsion of sublimate of silver and May water, grinding the sublimate for nine days with clean spittle and a little quicksilver, boiling it down by a third until it is so strong that it is not fit to be used, and with it the accursed woman removes wrinkles from her breasts and face. She makes, besides, a water of the whites of eggs and myrrh, camphor, *angelores*,[7] turpentine purified through three waters until it is as white as snow, and lily root and fine borax, and out of all this she concocts a mixture that makes her face shine like a sword. With the yolks she makes an oil for her hands, stirring in rose water and setting it to boil over a fire, and then with a clean cloth and a couple of sticks she skims off the oil which she uses to soften and clean her hands and face.

I do not say all this to teach such women, for they will not learn here what they have not learned already from other sources, but I say it to inform them that their secrets and tricks are known. Even John Boccaccio writes of the way women deck themselves out, and of their blemishes and how they conceal them, though not for long; and many others, among whom I am not worthy to be named, have written of and described these things. So be not astonished if I write from my personal experience, since John Boccaccio and many others have done so, as I have said.

What, then, will you find in a woman's chests? The Hours of St. Mary? The Lives of the Saints? The Psalter? Not a sign of them! On the contrary, you will find songs, sayings, verses, letters from their lovers, and many other follies, as well as beads, corals, ropes of mother-of-pearl, gold necklaces . . .[8] strung with precious stones, wigs, rolls of false hair, not to mention pumpkin and fenugreek seeds mixed with medlar for softening the hands, musk and civet for eyebrows and armpits, pulverized amber for the bath, to soften the flesh, as I have said, and cinnamon and cloves for the breath.

This is what you will find in their chests and cof-
fers, which are stuffed with an infinity of other
things which, if spread out, would stock a large
shop and one to be proud of. When they poke
about in them and put their things in order they get
as excited as if they were in Paradise—this from
their desire to have even more, because, even though
they had four times as much, they would not be sur-
feited or contented. All these things I have mentioned, acquired by good means or bad, vary according to the province and native costumes of each:
some from cities, others from the country, still others from the villages or the mountains, each according to the kingdom or country where she was born
and its dress and usages. Let him who understands
me take the particular example for the universal,
and he may be sure that there is no fraud, theft, or
villainy that a wicked woman will not perpetrate to
acquire these fineries, even against her own husband
or anyone else. We may conclude, therefore, that
it is a general rule that a woman will take anything,
regardless of where it comes from, or whether she
pleases God or offends Him with her goings-on.
Let her understand me who will, and, if she should
speak ill of me, may God forgive her!

CHAPTER FOUR

↱ *How woman is envious of all more
beautiful than she*

To doubt that the wicked woman is envious would
be to sin against the Holy Ghost, for every woman,
when she sees another more comely than she, is like

to die of envy. And I make no exception of mother against daughter, sister against sister, or cousin against cousin, for out of pure envy they gnaw their lips and scold like hoot owls. One will pretend that she is the more likely wench and does not imitate the other. Oh, no! But she studies the other's airs to steal them from her, her tricks of walking and talking, and still she thinks she is the more comely— all this from envy. And if the other is fair and she dark, she says: "By my faith, blessed is the black earth that yields the noble wheat! There's more virtue in a grain of black pepper than in a whole pound of white rice!"

But if the other is dark and she fair, then she really lets herself go. She says: "They think What's-her-name is beautiful! Lord, Lord, what a fine thing it is to have friends! But they haven't seen her as I did the other day, naked in the bath! Why, she's blacker than a devil, and so skinny that she looks like nothing so much as a skeleton! Her hair is as black as tar, her head huge, her neck short and thick as a bull's, her bosom all bone! Her breasts dangle like a goat's! She's straight up and down—no figure at all, flat! Her legs are spindly as a stork's, her feet lumpish. At the bath the other day the filthy thing hawked and spat until most of us were sick! There's not one good thing about her! If you're looking for wit and fun, seek it elsewhere. The shameless, slovenly slattern! She can't do fancywork or sew, except with coarse stitches. She can spin, but not fine. She's good for nothing but the bed! Look at the beauty! Go serve her, for she comes from high-toned people, she does! Go with her; don't let her walk alone! Her one-eyed grandfather dreamed her up,

or her father, Pedro Pérez the cobbler, won her
stretching hides with his teeth! And her mother!
Many a time the old crone has come to my house
peddling hair nets! And now look at her daughter
put on airs! As if we didn't know her! Look how
she gets herself up! But if you could see her house!
Ill swept, worse sprinkled, overflowing with spiders
and full of dust! There's beauty for you! Pfui and
pfui again! Well, now you've seen her and have
got something to talk about. God made us all, I
suppose, but one wonders. Look and listen, but if
you see anything don't talk about it. She's as black
as an eclipse! She's as white as my luck was the day
I was born! Upon my word, she smears whiting up
to her very eyes, and paint, no end! Her eyebrows
well plucked, high and arched, her eyes darkened
with kohl, her face peeled of its long and short
hairs with a mixture of turpentine and oil of camo-
mile; her lips a bright red, not naturally, of course,
but stained with fumitory seeds mixed with brazil
wood and alum; her teeth *anosegados* or scrubbed
with *manbre*,[9] the herb they call Indian; her nails
tinted with henna, longer than the claws of a hawk
or a falcon, so long that she has to wear gold braces
on them; her face shining like a sword with all those
washes I spoke of. She applies packs to her face, one
after the other, for ten days running, because when
she doesn't she's as black as a Moor of the Indies.
She makes them with an ointment of the juice of
radish leaves, sugar, and Cyprian soap, oil of al-
monds and French beans cooked with cow's gall."
These and a thousand other kinds of packs women
wear for nine days on end, and they stink like the
devil with all the things they smear on their faces

to refine their complexions, along with gelatin mixed with beans well ground.

"That is why she is so gaped at, as if she were an altar and the source of all beauty! And you tell me she is beautiful! By my faith, may God give her beauty! She is beautiful who, with only a linen kerchief on her head and no other ornament, shines like a star. That's what I do. Nothing but water from yon river ever touches this face, and I would have you know I am no less worth looking at than she, with all her make-up! I say more, that if I were a man I'd see myself hanged before I'd lie with such! O Lord God, why didst Thou not make me a man, for I'd be damned if I'd suffer a single night for such a woman, or even leave my house for her! Lord, Lord, why dost Thou deprive men of their senses? But there are eyes that like to look at eyesores, for, as the proverb has it: *Birds of a feather flock together*. Well, by God and my soul, may I burst if I don't sit near her at church next Sunday! We'll see then, we'll see who takes the prize! Burn me if I don't go in with drums beating! I'll take her airs from her, by this mark that God gave me! You'll see how she rages when I come in! By my faith I'll do it!"

This is what women are used to saying of one another, all from pure envy. I say, moreover, that once a woman has worn her jewels, clothes, and finery, she no longer cares for them and cannot stand the sight of them the next day, if she can get the money to buy new ones, such is her inextinguishable and insatiable appetite. Rather, she covets everything she sees other women wearing, even though it is not as good as hers. As soon as she sees

something different she must have it and wear it,
for, as the old proverb has it: *What a fine garden
is my neighbor's! What a fine cock she has!* But
as soon as a woman has worn a thing of her own,
even once, it has no longer any value in her eyes.
Whatever belongs to her neighbor is pure gold;
whatever is hers is mud and ashes. Such is her
unbridled cupidity, difficult to quench and impossible to diminish.

If by chance her neighbor is so beautiful that she
cannot dispraise her, since her beauty is manifest
to all the world, at that point she begins to wag her
head and roll her eyes and twist her mouth, and she
says: "Well, she is beautiful no doubt, but not so
much as you give her credit for. Is she the only
beautiful woman you've ever seen? Well, really!
God help us! Indeed! What's the matter with you?
Oho, what a miracle! As if we had never seen her
equal! What a lot of wonders you've seen and
miracles that don't amount to a row of pins! Oh,
she's beautiful enough. A woman is certainly beautiful if she's got a good figure, but I know a thing
or two about that, and I'll say no more. If I only
dared to speak. . . . Well, I will speak, because I'd
burst if I didn't, by God! I saw her the other day,
this one you think is so beautiful and praise so much,
I saw her talking with an abbot, and giggling and
frolicking with him in his house, and pinching him
and sticking him with pins, and shrieking with
laughter! Upon my word, that's what I saw, and
I won't say another word, because the abbot's red
face didn't come from saying matins, nor did hers
from spinning at her wheel! God's wrath! Good
women would not be seen among those scoundrels,

by God! The devil take such goings-on! How many
poor wretches of men do such wicked women snare
with their paint and powder! So you think What's-
her-name is beautiful, do you? She can have her
beauty! Much good may her stuck-up ways do her!
Just look at her carry on! Beautiful, is she? Beautiful? St. Mary is beautiful! But I wouldn't be in her
shoes with all her beauty! For God's sake, my
friend, don't come at me with such beauties! If she
is beautiful let her be so; it's all one to me! Did you
ever hear such a lot of talk about nothing! You
want to make a knight out of a flea, and out of this
creature who sneaks about in corners with abbots
you want to make a great beauty! Don't talk to me
about her, for by God's Passion I'd burst with rage
just from hearing it! For God's sake let's go eat
and leave off this nonsense, for we can get along
better without it than without food! Pfui, my friend!
Jesus, what a foolish business! What a lot of fuss
about nothing!"

Meanwhile, it is impossible for her really to say
anything good about another woman, or praise her,
for if she says one good thing she turns round and
says ten times as much evil. Moreover, you will find
few women who, out of pure envy, can check their
tongues, for the wretched creatures think that by
dispraising others they make themselves beautiful,
and by dishonoring others they enhance their own
honor.

The envious and backbiting detractor, that speaker
of evil, that two-edged sword, who praises a man
to his face and tears him to pieces behind his back
—if this fellow, I say, only knew what the wise
think of him and how they know him for what he

is, he would burst! How many of us, for our sins, play at this game nowadays! The wise hold such a one in scant esteem and despise his learning, and his good name suffers among the discreet. Therefore, the loud talker, the scorner, the backbiter, the speaker of evil, the mocker, the gossip, the jester, let him console himself with the thought that, although he mocks many, many mock and laugh at him! This is his punishment and it is fitting that he should suffer it, as he will. As Petrarch says, in his *De Remediis utriusque fortunae:* "He is a wise man who, being obliged to bear a burden, bears it cheerfully."

Let many take this lesson to heart, especially women, who know what burdens they must bear when they give themselves to men in concubinage, love, or marriage, for they yield up their liberty, in one degree or another, to him to whom they submit themselves. It is folly, therefore, to kick against the pricks. And the same holds true for a vassal against his lord, the servant against his master, a subject against his conqueror, the lowly against those of higher station, for, as the wise one says: "We cannot make ourselves the equals of those who are more powerful." This is where an infinite number of men come to grief who refuse to recognize authority or grant superiority to those whom Our Lord made greater, stronger, and of higher station than they. It does not matter that the great achieved their authority through favor or merit, or even that they neglected to do good works; in any case God granted to such men and women the privilege of being desired, great, loved, powerful, and of high station. And if it seems at times that they abuse their power, for the sins of their subjects, well, sometimes men seek the cause of their own undoing. That is how God ordained it, but some people do not like it and will not put up with it, but prefer to dash their heads against the wall. Let every man and woman, therefore, consider how wise it is to obey one's superiors and betters, for the contrary is folly. And let a man consider whether he profits himself, when an inferior pits himself against his superior, for in the end he must submit willy-nilly and is the more dishonored, for what he could once have done graciously brings him no thanks when he does it.

So then, to resume our argument, many do a great deal of idle talking when they would do more wisely to keep their mouths shut. In like fashion you will see women who in a single hour utter a thousand scurrilous remarks, evil-speaking and back-biting, for they would burst if they kept silent. If, on the other hand, they hear themselves praised, like a river they get all roiled up, and the wily anglers may then fish in troubled waters, catching the silly creatures in a net of flattery, using this kind of bait: "Oh, what a beautiful woman! How lovely! How fetching! You're the prettiest creature in the world!" And the mad or ill-advised idiots believe it all, little thinking that the flatterer is lying doubly: lying, knowing perfectly well it is not so, and lying to deceive, swearing that it is.

Oh, mad and senseless woman, weak of understanding and lacking in natural judgment! Believe me, and doubt it not, that he who praises you deceives you. As Cato says: "Sweetly pipes the flute when the hunter, sweetly piping, snares the bird." Let her consider how she can be snared with sweet

words, not with harsh ones. Thus only at the beginning, for she learns later what she is in for, because
it is pleasant to enter the net, but to remain is bitter.
Her entrance is like honey, her life afterward like
gall. As Solomon says: "Better is the end of a thing
than the beginning thereof." Thus, many things
have a good beginning but a different ending. As
the proverb has it: *He who fails to look forward
will fall backward.* Let each one, therefore, heed
what he says or does, for a word is like a stone
which, once it has left one's hand, cares not where
it strikes. Or, as the wise one says: "Words have
wings and, once uttered, cannot be recalled. You
may deny them indeed, but you may not unsay
them." Oh, how much harm comes to men from
talking too much and, above all, talking when they
should keep silence! We may conclude, therefore,
that envy is the source of these and other things
that women say about each other, heedless of the
proverb: *I heard, I saw, and kept my mouth shut,
for I wish to live in peace.*

CHAPTER FIVE

⌐ *How woman's constancy depends upon
what you give her*

It is not to be marveled at that a wicked woman is
neither firm nor constant in her actions and words,
for her firmness and constancy are not so great that
if a man pursues her diligently he will not get her
to yield, a woman being like wax, very ready to
receive new impressions. Just as wax will take the
form of any seal, great or small, well or ill cut, so

will a wicked woman mould herself to the liking of anyone at all. If you look for love, you will find it; if you give her gifts, leave her not; if you do not, be on your way. She will neglect her grinding, her baking, and her honor; she puts first things last, and last things first; everything depends on money. Moreover, a woman will tell you one thing today and an hour later something else; if she says yes to one, she says no to another; she will give her word to one and stick pins in another; she winks at one and stares at the next; she nudges one with her foot and pokes the next with her elbow; she presses your hand and turns away her face. Then, the signs she can make with her eyes are many: she can make a fool of a man by looking at him, or mock him, or flatter him, or make him fall in love with her; she can slay with a glance, or let on she is angry or furious by showing the whites of her eyes. She can do more tricks with her eyes than a prestidigitator with his hands. And with her mouth she is really expert! These airs that she puts on are like a weather vane to tell the knowing how the wind blows: now east, now west, now north, now south.

Do not think, therefore, that any woman in the world can assure you that she will not change in the next moment, because she cannot stay fixed in purpose for a single hour, and she says: "This looks all right to me, but if that happens then I think this other will be better. No, it's worse. What would become of me in that case? No, I wouldn't do that for the world! Upon my word, I'll do it! No, I won't. Yes, I will. Isabel, fetch me two green leaves from the olive tree. Throw them into the fire, you daughter of a whore, and if they both land face up or face down, I'll do it, I promise. But if one lands face up and the other face down, it's a bad sign. May I be burned if I do it, amen! But if one jumps up and lands on top of the other, aha, that's a sign of love and evil will never touch me! I'll do it!"

There is an infinity of these and other things that I shall refrain from describing here, lest I teach these good merchants how to peddle their wares. This is why they believe in sneezes and dreams, auguries and signs. And this is why they run and cast spells and love charms, and commit other abominations, for the devil is a good fisherman and with a small worm will catch a fat eel. The evil one begins by pretending to do good in the service of God, teaching us to love and cherish, and that it is good for the husband to love his wife and a holy thing to abhor other women and love only his own. This is the way the devil begins. Then, when he has them hooked, he turns the page and does abominable things to his victims, making them deny their Creator and lose what He desires for us. Thus, although the beginning is good and holy, the end is evil and hellish. And so, with an olive leaf or a sneeze, you begin to believe in such things, and then little by little you will turn into a necromancer and enchanter, a wizard or a diviner or a soothsayer. Let each man, therefore, beware of the beginning, if he would end as he desires. And women get into this kind of thing because of their "Yes, I will; no, I won't; I'll say thus-and-so; no, I won't." They play ball with their wits, and that is why the wise Marcianus said: "It would be easier to create a new world than to change a woman's ways."

Do not trust a woman's word, therefore, any

farther than from your hand to your purse. If she promises you something, run and get a bag; but if you are not sure of what she promises—that is, if you do not have her in your power or under your orders, and even if you have—do not think that you have got her fast, but still be ready with your gifts. In this follow the ancient proverbs: *Be not slow in taking, for many things are lost in delay;* and, *If you are given a kid, run for a rope;* and, *If anyone promises you something, seize it at once.* For you will see by experience that if you fail to take immediately what a woman offers you, or if you let time go by, she will go back on her word, for she changes her mind a thousand times an hour. If she does promise you something, such is her avarice and such her inconstancy that she will revoke her promise, out of shame at having promised at all. She will mull it over a thousand times; she turns and twists and thinks how she can get out of it plausibly, and whether she can put you off with a penny in the hope of getting a florin. Nuns are most adept at this, although it would not be proper to single them out, for they are also women and must be included in the general rule, with praise for good and honest nuns, and reproof for the wicked (if there are any such). But because nuns are kept cloistered and apart, I lift my pen here, because I must rather than because I wish to, for I see that my angry pen had something to say in this matter, but, as the Decretal says: "It is not good to add affliction to the afflicted, but one should take pity on them in their misery." Therefore, those who are not free, but are cloistered and under the discipline of others, have enough to put up with already, for, although a nun may wish to sleep, she is obliged to stay awake; she may wish to eat, but they make her fast and do public penance by eating on the floor. Item: she is scourged, and, if she wishes to go out, she is forced to stay in, and an infinity of other things. So one should not speak of those who suffer daily under the authority of others.

In conclusion, then, I say that beyond a doubt woman is entirely fickle in giving and promising, and in other things. I beg you, therefore, not to let yourself get snared by one who promises and shamelessly goes back on her word, and to take only from Him who generously promises eternal life, although you deserve it not.

CHAPTER SIX

⌐ *How woman is two-faced*

It is not to be doubted that woman has two faces, or is a double-edged knife, for we see every day that she says one thing with her mouth, but has something different in her heart. There is not a man alive who, no matter how close a friend, or how old or intimate, he may be of a woman, can know her secret thoughts, or get her to talk openly and honestly with him. She watches every approach, fears every moment, guards every corner of her heart, reveals no secret, and allows no man to discover her will and desire, lest she be subjected to him. She will swear and swear again: "I never did such a thing! I never said such a thing! I never pretended such a thing! I swear by this, that, and the other that I was never mixed up in it or knew anything about it! Don't you believe me? Tell me you believe me." And if you do not, listen to her now: "Oh you lump! You thick-skinned ox! You stick! You devil! Tell me, you do believe me, don't you? Well, I don't care whether you do or not, but may I be burned if I ever said such a thing, or even mentioned it, amen! May I go to hell if I did! May the devil fly away with me! May he strangle me! May he take my soul! May I never see Paradise! May I have no joy on earth! May I see my children grow up to be servants! May my soul go to perdition! May I never have any honor but what I was born with! May I never enjoy him I love most dearly! May I never get married! May God take His light from me! May God never help me! May I never see my son an archbishop! May God never grant my prayers! May I never enjoy you! May tumors, an evil death, pain in the side, strike me and kill me and take me from this world! By the sign of the Cross! By the Virgin Mary! By God Almighty! By the Passion of Christ! By the true and living God!"

Other women have different ways of swearing: "By my life as an honest woman! By my life! By your life! By my son's life! By the repose of your good father whom I knew (may he rest in peace)! I swear by my life! I hope to die! May my father never love me! May I be paraded through the streets like her who got whipped! May I see my children hanged! By the king's life! By Our Lord! May I be stricken with grief! May I never live out the year! May God give you health and me my deserts! By the life of Juan González! I have sworn!"

These and an infinity of other oaths women swear ordinarily, but, when they swear, they do so in two ways: they swear with their mouths and revoke it in their hearts, saying: "Let a bad oath fall upon stones!" Or, when they say: "May I never see pleasure again!" they say to themselves: "Well, not quite never!" In this way they think they are deceiving others, but they deceive only themselves, for he who swears falsely commits perjury. Hence these women who swear one thing and do another are called two-faced, or double-edged knives: they show one thing and hide another; they preach one thing and practice another. Is there a worse folly in the world than to believe a false woman when she swears? Or to hold her innocent who would rob her own father? Or to take for truth the lies told by a flatterer? Or to believe in the honesty of a wicked woman when she swears? Or in the friendship of a spiteful one? Or to believe the falsehoods of a lying woman?

Learn, moreover, to do unto her what she does unto you. Since she does not reveal her secret thoughts to you, do not reveal yours to her, for you have heard what happened to men in ancient times, and even to those now living, who revealed their heart's secrets. Take the case of Samson, how he revealed to his wife, Delilah, that his strength lay in his hair, and how she, while combing it and picking fleas from it, cut it off while he was asleep and delivered him up to his enemies, and how, when he tried to arm himself, he found he had no strength, and so they blinded him and dragged him to the market places and squares and wedding festivals, mocking him and saying: "What do you think of him now? Look, the fierce bull is turned into a sheep!" And this went on until one day, when many people were gathered at a festival, he had a boy lead him to a pillar in the middle of the house, his hair having grown out again since he had been shorn and he having regained his strength. So he tumbled

the house to the ground, and he and all who were
in it died, to the number of five thousand, and he
said: "Here Samson will die, and all who are with
him!" Thus in his despair he chose to die, seeing
how low he had fallen, and all because he had revealed his secret to his wife.

Let each man, therefore, be on his guard and learn
from women, for, although they are great chatterboxes, they are closemouthed enough about their
own secrets. So imitate them in this, for, as Cato
says: "Thus you will deceive the one who would
deceive you." At least by some such device you will
be able easily to defend yourself, for bear in mind
that what a woman desires is to learn, discover, and
know your secret thoughts, and she will scratch
about, like a hen scratching for worms, and for two
hours on end she will tease you, saying: "Tell me
now; tell me, won't you?" This with embraces,
flattery, and kisses, and when she has exhausted this
vein she will say: "Don't drive me frantic! Don't
make me lose my temper! You're killing me! Don't
upset my stomach! Don't give me a bellyache! For
God's sake tell me! Wretch that I am, miserable and
unlucky! Oh, what a lump you are! Why do you
act like that? Oh, what a boor! I'll have something
to say about this! Tell me now, for God's sake, by
my soul and body! Well, if you won't, I give you
my word I'll never speak to you again! Won't you,
won't you, won't you tell me?" And at the third
"Won't you" she will say: "Oh, go away and leave
me in peace!" And she lifts her eyebrows and squats
on the ground, her hand on her cheek, morose and
even weeping with rage, red as a pomegranate,
sweating like a galley slave, her heart pounding like
that of a lioness, while she gnaws her lips and stares

fiercely at you. If you speak to her she will refuse to answer; if you touch her she will turn her back, saying: "Get out! I know how you love me! I believed you once and I've regretted it ever since!" Then she will pretend to sigh, although she has no desire to.

Then, perhaps, the poor spiritless nincompoop will say: "Don't be angry; I'll tell you." So he tells her all his secret thoughts, and she pretends to value them not at all and scorns to listen to them, because he had not told her in the first place; but even as she turns away her face she bends her ear, and when the silly fool has emptied himself of everything he knows, the prying busybody will say: "Is that your secret? Well, I knew that already! Go try that bone on another dog! Do you take me for a fool? Be on your way and tell your lies to some other woman, not me! Look out for me, and God help you! What a secret! What a foolishness, by this mark that God gave me! But look out for me! That's all I've got to say!"

This is how they get their way, thinking one thing and saying another, from which we may conclude that woman is a double-dealer. Therefore, let God understand them who can, and let him deal with them who has the power to do so!

CHAPTER SEVEN

⌐ *Of disobedience in wives*

That wives are disobedient admits of no doubt whatever. If you command your wife to do something, be sure that she will do entirely the contrary. This is a fixed rule. The wise Ptolemy said truly, speaking of wives: "If you order your wife to do what is forbidden, she will do the opposite." To illustrate the matter further I will cite a few examples.

There was once a very learned man of the East, of the city of Salustra in the kingdom of Scotland,[10] who had a beautiful wife of illustrious lineage. She, made haughty by her beauty—as, for their sins, happens with some women today—committed adultery against her husband, being loved and sought after by many. This she did so frequently that some smoke had to appear from so much fire. The good man became aware of his misfortunes, but, acting wisely, unlike those who dash their heads against the wall, he waited one, ten, and twenty days, wondering how he could remedy this evil. And he thought to himself: "If I kill her I will ruin myself, for she has two things on her side: justice and her kinsmen, who will proceed against me; justice, because no man should take the law into his own hands without knowledge of it and without proper witnesses, worthy of credence, and good depositions, with notarized instruments and documents—all this in the presence of the president, governor, magistrate, or regent of the king's court. Moreover, one ought not avenge himself or punish anyone at all by his own hand. I cannot, therefore, proceed without depositions, for her kinsmen would say, besides, that I brought these charges in order to kill her and take another wife, and they would be my enemies."

In view of all this and of all the evils and harm that might ensue, he did not wish to kill her by his own hand, lest he himself be destroyed; nor did he wish to kill her by recourse to the law, lest his good name suffer. He was discreet and acted in accordance with the uses of this world, although according to God he chose the worse. So he planned to get rid of her in such wise that he would he held innocent in the sight of men, although not in the sight of God, because, as I have said, he who is the cause of evil, or who allows it to be done with his knowledge, is held accountable. Thus he preferred to have her seem to be the cause of her own death. Accordingly, he had some poison made which he mixed into the best and most fragrant wine he could obtain, for she was not indifferent to good wine. And he poured it into a flask and said to himself: "If I put this flask where she will see it, even though I say to her: 'Beware of tasting this,' she, being a woman, will disobey me and surely drink it, and so die." And so he did: the good wise man put the flask in a window where she would see it, and she said at once: "What is that, husband?" And he answered: "Wife, it is a flask, but I command and beseech you not to taste what is in it, because if you do so you will die forthwith, just as Our Lord said to Eve." This he said in the presence of all his household, so that they would be witnesses. Then he made as if to go away, but he had hardly reached the door when she seized the flask and said: "Upon my word, may I be burned if I don't find out what this is!" She smelled the flask and saw that it was filled with good wine, and said: "Oho! What a fine husband I've got! So this is what he told me not to taste! May I be damned if I'll put up with it! He'll not be the only one to drink it, God willing, for not all good things are for the king's mouth." Thereupon she put the flask to her lips and drank a little, and at once fell dead. And when the husband heard the shouting he said to himself: "She is done for!" But he ran in plucking his beard and crying: "Oh, woe is me!" But to himself he said: "Why didn't I do it sooner?" Aloud he said: "Alas, what will become of me, poor wretch?" But in his heart: "What if this traitor isn't dead?" So he went to her and shook her, thinking she might be alive, but she was dead.

See, then, how a wife, just because she would not obey, did what she had been forbidden to do, and so died, as others have for the same reason.

Another wife did much the same thing, having wronged her husband, and he said to himself: "Wait a bit and I'll fix you!" So he had a chest made with three locks, and inside it he placed a steel crossbow and cocked it, so placing it that if anyone should open the chest the arrow would strike him in the heart. He brought the chest to his house and said: "Wife, I beg you not to open this chest, for if you do you will die at once. Don't forget that I am so commanding you in the presence of all these people, and, as God is my witness, if you disobey me you will rue it, and I say no more." So saying he went about his business. As soon as he was gone his wife began to worry about it, one day, another day, one night, ten nights, until she was bursting with vexation and even got such an upset stomach that she could not stand it. So she said to herself one day: "May I be damned if my husband hasn't got some secret in that chest that he doesn't want me to see, he has put so many locks on it and forbidden me to open it! Well, he can't do that to me! Even if I die for it I'm going to open the chest and see what's in it!" So she opened it, and when she lifted the lid the crossbow discharged and the arrow struck her in the breast and killed her.

Thus you see how a wife will die, even, or burst, to do what she has been forbidden to do.

Another wife was very disputatious and with her arguing made her husband's life miserable. So one day he decided that all this arguing of hers would bring him to his grave, and he said to her: "Wife, tomorrow I have invited some friends in for supper. Set the table for them in the garden on the bank of the river, under the big pear tree, so we can enjoy ourselves." The wife did so: she set the table and cooked a good supper, and they sat down to eat. The roast chickens were brought in and the husband said: "Wife, hand me the knife that you have stuck in your belt, for this one of mine will hardly cut dough." And she replied: "What's the matter with you, my friend? It's not a knife, but scissors, scissors!" When the husband saw that she was arguing unnecessarily he said: "God deliver me from this wicked female! Even in my pleasure she argues with me!" So saying, he kicked her into the river. And she began to flounder about under the water, but she resolved not to yield, even though she drowned: dead but unconquered! So she raised her two fingers above the water and wriggled them like a pair of scissors, giving her husband to understand that they were still scissors, and she was carried off down the river drowning. The guests, struck with pity for her, set off running downstream to rescue her, but the husband began to shout: "Come back, my friends, come back! Where are you going? And didn't you know that my wife is so stubborn she will even argue with the river and make her way upstream in spite of the current?" And while they turned back, thinking he was speaking seriously, the stubborn wife, with her accursed stubbornness, still arguing, came to a bad end.

Another wife was going on a pilgrimage with her husband. They sat down in the shade of a poplar tree and, while they were resting, a thrush burst into song, and the husband said: "God bless you! Do you hear, wife, how the thrush is singing?" And she replied: "But don't you see by its feathers and its small head that it's not a thrush but a throstle?" Said the husband: "You fool! Don't you see by the color of its neck and its long tail that it's a thrush and nothing but a thrush?" But she said: "And don't you see by its song and the way it wags its head that it can't be anything but a throstle?" Said the husband: "Go to the devil, you pigheaded idiot! It's a thrush!" His wife answered: "By God and my soul, I say it's a throstle." Then said the husband: "The devil must have brought that thrush here!" And she replied: "By the Virgin Mary, it's a throstle!" Then the husband, in a rage, took the stick he used on the donkey and broke her arm with it, so, instead of going on a pilgrimage to pray St. Mary to give them the son they wanted, they returned to a hermitage to pray St. Anthony to heal the stupid woman's arm she had broken by arguing.

I could tell you of a thousand cases like these, but so many of them happen every day that it would be a waste of time. To conclude, then, experience demonstrates that wives are stubborn and disobedient and always say and do the opposite of what they are told.

CHAPTER EIGHT

↰ *How proud woman cares not what she says or does*

It is a general rule that woman is proud. Just watch a woman when she is angry, for she will say things with that infernal mouth of hers that should not be heard or listened to. Indeed, I hold him to be a wise and worthy man who, when he sees an angry woman, flies her tirades and turns his back on her and lets her talk until she runs down. If he does not answer her she soon stops, but if he winds her up, such is her folly and lack of sense that she will not check her tongue but will spew out everything she knows about herself as well as her neighbors, because not for anything in the world would she stop her mouth. Still less will she stop her hands if she has anything to use them on, for a cat is not more eager after liver than a woman is to grab. And if at that moment she gets hold of some secret or other, even a deadly one, she will tell it at once or die trying— in this she knows no restraint.

Let each man, therefore, if he has any sense, look after himself and yield to her, and keep silence, unless he is mad. This is why women are so bold and fear men not at all, for they protect themselves by saying: "I am a woman; he won't molest me; he won't strike me or draw his sword against me, for I am a woman and he would be dishonored if he did such a thing, because a man should not attack or use force on a woman, Jew, or priest, for they are weak and helpless creatures." And this is why a woman will frequently dare to dishonor, vilify, or defame a man, knowing that he, for shame or good sense, will not raise his hand against her, although she knows well enough that the most valiant woman would not be able to stand against the most cowardly man. Even so, God help us, she is sometimes mistaken, for, although a man of sense will not take a bold line with her, some other may come along and say to her: "I'm glad to see you, and take that now! Excuse my haste, but I've got a little matter to attend to. Sorry I didn't recognize you!"

Lord, Lord, what a deal of trouble a woman will get into for this reason alone! For she will presume: "He wouldn't dare! He wouldn't be so crazy! He wouldn't have the nerve! I know he won't chance it!" So her mouth gets her into trouble, for there is not an angel that a woman would not make a devil of, nor a man she would not make deny himself, with that pride of hers! So proud is she that a fierce lion is more easily tamed, for even if you had her tied hand and foot, you could kill her before she would surrender or retract. Such is her nature that, however slight an insult you offer her, she flies into such a rage that she is like to burst and is in a fury to get her revenge at once. Besides, so great is her pride that she has no respect for any other woman whatever; rather, she scorns them all and esteems them not at all. One she calls low; another filthy; another of no account; another lazy; another slovenly; another wicked; another a backbiter, and she herself is perhaps worse than any of them. She finds faults in others, but not in herself. She was begotten by the Holy Ghost, she was! And there is no woman who does not despise all others, such is her pride and arrogance. Moreover, I say that there is not a mad wench or a dishonest old woman who does not reveal in her actions that she is boastful, proud, and puffed up with conceit. And if the world tolerates these things somewhat in a young woman, is that any reason for tolerating them in an old woman who is in league with the devil? Why, indeed, if, when an old woman is decked out in her finery and is well plucked and peeled, she looks like a boned monkey! She looks down at her breasts. Breasts, did I say? I call them rather bags of bones! She looks at her hands all covered with rings, and chews her lips to make them red, casting her eyes about, looking sideways, wriggling her bottom like mad, looking at the others, and smiling and making jokes about all the men and women she passes.

A single one of these ancient gulls needs a whole square to strut about in, with a long train of women behind her and many men in front. "Marica, you daughter of a whore, hold my skirt for me!" At times, as if by accident, she will raise her skirt and show a slipper or a foot or a bit of leg, and then she will look around to see if anyone is watching. And she will pretend that she had only been careless and will drop her skirt and lower her eyes modestly. But she knows well enough what she is doing! And if she is at home clad only in a wrapper, she will lean over and pick up something from the floor, to show her shanks proudly and a great expanse of buttocks, this to attract the attention of whoever is looking at her, or of the one she would be desired by. As the wise Ptolemy says: "Pride and haughtiness go with beauty. A man or woman endowed with beauty and a fine body is proud and haughty." Read Petrarch, in his *De remediis*, Book II, *De dolore*, where he says: "If Helen had not been so beautiful the walls of Troy would still be standing." Etc.

It is, therefore, much better to make oneself

beautiful with virtues than to be born beautiful, for a large man can dwell in a small house, and a great and virtuous heart in a small body. Only true virtue is free, but vice is committed to every evil. A man of twisted mind is difficult to straighten, and a wicked woman is hard to teach and very averse to abandoning her vices. Hence it is clear that it is impossible to change a woman's ways. As a certain wise man said: "When pride occurs in good women it corrupts them." Therefore, there is no man or woman, however endowed with virtues, who will not lose them if they do not cast out pride; nor will their virtues avail them. So then, we may conclude from the above that woman is born with great pride, and that he who has the least to do with her will be doing God a signal service.

CHAPTER NINE

⌐ *How woman is given to windy boastfulness*

The whole trouble comes from a woman's inordinate love of boasting, for, with few exceptions, there is not a woman in the world who can resist boasting and blowing about her finery and beauty; nor is there one who does not believe all the words spoken in praise of her, even though false, for she presumes they are all true. I am not astonished at this blemish in females, for they get it naturally from their Mother Eve, who believed the serpent, the devil Satan, who deceived her, saying: "If you will eat of the fruit of the tree of knowledge of good and evil, you will be equal in wisdom to the All Highest who made you." Then she, because of her weak understanding and great vainglory, believed that Lucifer was equal in wisdom to Him whose wisdom is without equal, and that if she were equal to Him in wisdom she would forthwith be His equal in power. So she did what she had been forbidden to do: she tasted of the fruit. Thus did man and woman fall and bring down with them their descendants, for women were, still are, and always will be the same, in seeking vaingloriously to be great, powerful, feared—such is their great vainglory. I say moreover that there is not a woman alive today who can get her fill of being gaped at, desired, and sighed after, and praised and talked about in public. This is her desire, her mania, her god: pleasure, delight, and merrymaking. So her life is made up of going about all decked out in finery, with the greatest possible show and ostentation; and when she is gaped at, sighed after, or talked about, or sneered at in the street, she will pretend to be annoyed and will put on a sour look, as if impatient. But God knows the truth of the matter, which is that these are only gentle mule kicks, because the only thing such a woman wishes is to be desired, talked about, and even jeered at, even though she will say: "Did you ever see such a fool? Such a lunatic? Such a simpleton?" This she says with a straight face, but under her mantle she is laughing like mad. On the other hand, if she appears and is not noticed, she is like to burst with rage; but if she is noticed she is a different person, grimacing and gesticulating more than a novice jouster. All this comes from her vainglory and her desire to show off.

A daughter will say to her mother, a wife to her husband, a cousin to her cousin, a mistress to her lover: "I feel just terrible! My head aches, I hurt all over, my stomach is upset, from being cooped up inside these four walls. I want to go to confession at the Franciscan church; I want to go to Mass at St. Dominic's. There's a Passion Play at the Carmelites'. Let's go see the Augustinian monastery, it's so beautiful! Let's go by way of the Church of the Trinity and see the helmet of St. Blas and watch all those fat priests strolling about. Lord, what thick necks they have! How fat! How rich and well dressed! Let's go hear the sermon at St. Mary's of Grace."

All this gadding about, wherever she happens to be, is merely to get herself gaped at and admired. But it's worse when she has no finery to wear, or a maid to go with her, and she says: "Marica, go to my cousin's house and borrow her scarlet skirt. Juanilla, go to my sister's and get her to lend me her Moorish *aljuba*, the green one of Florentine silk. Inesica, go to my gossip's and borrow her hair net and arm band. Catalinilla, go to my neighbor's and borrow her girdle and gold earrings. Francisquilla, go to Madame What's-her-name's and borrow her gold rosary. Teresuela, run to my niece's and borrow her silk cape, the one lined with marten. Mencihuela, go at once to the perfumer's or the merchant's and get me some whiting and two ounces of cinnamon, and some cloves for my breath."

They borrow these and other things, some more, some less, each according to her estate. Some lack one thing and some lack several, and others lack the whole outfit. Why, they even borrow servants and maids! And if a woman wishes to ride she will borrow a mule, a boy to carry her train, and two or three or four footmen to walk beside her and keep her from falling off—they in mud up to their knees and dead with the cold, or, in summer, sweating like pigs with fatigue, trotting after her, holding her on, and she making a show of falling off so they will come and support her. And she puts a hand on the shoulder of one, her other hand on the head of another, her arms outspread like the wings of a setting hen, and she rising up in the saddle whenever she sees someone gaping at her, twisting her mouth, sometimes complaining, sometimes groaning, and she says: "Hold me, I'm falling! Lord, what a bad saddle! Lord, what a mule! I'm shaken to a jelly! It trots and doesn't know how to walk! My hand hurts from holding it back, poor wretch that I am! I'm beaten to a pulp! What will become of me?" And so she goes her way wailing like a Magdalene.

But if some squire takes her rein and leads her, and there are people about to see her, then she will say: "Oh, my friends, straighten my skirt for me. Please adjust my stirrup. Oh dear, my saddle is slipping!" This so that they will stay with her and gape, and all from her vainglory, pride, and desire to show off.

Many such parade through the streets in their finery, and when they get home and return what they have borrowed, all they have left is a lot of ragged, worn-out, ripped, filthy, and ill-fitting clothes that look as though they were bought secondhand. Who would recognize them at home who saw them in the street? They make do with bread and onions, cheese and radishes, and lucky at that; but in the street they let on that all is gold that glisters.

I could tell you even worse things about them, for they pretend to their neighbors that they are made of money; but their gold turns into dross and poverty and ragged skirts, and then back they go to their tears and distaff and spinning wheel, making nets, fancywork, embroidery, winding sheets, purses, pillows, fruit covers, and handkerchiefs; knitting blouses, making arm bands and many other things, and even so they are lucky to find work, although they earn only tenpence a day. Ah, but you should have seen them with their squires, servants, maids, and footmen, bowing to everyone they met, letting on they were the wives of knights of twenty lances, or at least the daughters or nieces of such!

All this comes from their great vanity and little wit, because they would be praised, desired, and talked about. And there is no woman, however lowly her estate, who does not pretend that she is of the nobility, with great kinfolk and high connections—this from her vanity and lack of sense—not only outside her own province where she is a stranger, but even in the village where she was born and where she is better known than she knows herself; but those who hear of it keep silence for the sake of peace, or because it means nothing to them. This comes from her vanity and great folly. Thus we may conclude that a woman, with or without a dowry, is endowed with vainglory.

CHAPTER TEN

↱ *How woman perjures herself falsely swearing*

That a wicked woman is a liar it would be a sin to doubt, for there is not a woman who is not ready with a pack of lies and who will not twist the truth

—who, indeed, for a slight thing of no value will not swear a thousand oaths that she is not lying, and who for a very small gain or profit in anything she sees will fail to tell an infinity of lies. Hence you will see that the actions of most women are tricks and stratagems, colored and adorned with lies. At times, slyly lying, they will bear false witness and do wrong to other women. I do not know of a man, however clever and experienced he may be, who can make a woman admit she is lying; nor one, however quick-witted, who can keep her from turning the truth upside down by swearing and forswearing and cursing herself, and insisting that what he saw, and still sees with his own eyes, never happened.

I will give you an example of this, and I could give you a thousand. A woman had a man in her house when her husband came home unexpectedly, and she had to hide her lover behind a curtain. And when the husband came in he said: "What are you doing, wife?" And she answered: "Husband, I don't feel at all well." The husband sat down on a bench beside the bed and said: "Bring me something to eat." Meanwhile, the other, who was behind the curtain, dared not show himself, and she pretended that she had to go behind the curtain to get some linen, and said to him: "When I show my husband my breast come out, my friend, and be off." And so it happened. Said she: "Husband, you've no idea how my breast is swollen. I'm in agony with so much milk." And he said: "Let me see." Whereupon she took out her breast and shot a stream of milk into his eyes, completely blinding him, while the other escaped. And the husband said: "You daughter of a whore, how your milk smarts!" And the other who was making his escape said: "What can the poor cuckold do about it?" The husband heard the noise but could see nothing, and said: "Who was it passed by just now? I think I heard a man." And she said: "It was the cat, alas, running off with the meat!" So she set out running after the other, pretending she was chasing the cat, and locked the door and ran back to her husband, who could now see, but not the extent of his woe. This is how women are in the habit of bolstering up their lies with tricks.

I will give you another illustration. A woman had a friar hidden behind her bed, and when her husband came home she did not know how to get rid of him. So she went to her husband and said: "Where have you been that you got yourself all covered with hairs?" The husband turned his back so she could brush him, and the friar got away. And the husband said: "I think I heard a man just now." And she replied: "What's the matter with you? Are you out of your mind? Woe is me! Who is in the habit of coming here? You must be all upset from being with some mistress of yours, since you take the cat for a man! It's a sign of good times ahead!" The husband fell silent and said: "Hush, silly one! I said it only to test you." Thus the woman turned her lie into truth, as women still do.

Another woman had a man hidden one night, when her husband came home and she had to hide him under the bed. And when the husband came in she upset the lamp and it went out. Then she said to her husband: "Get me a match." And while he went to get it the other came out from under the bed and escaped through the stable.

Still another had a man hidden behind the curtain and wondered how she could get rid of him, for her husband would not leave the room, so she thought up the following trick. She went to the kitchen and got a new pot she had bought that day, and brought it to her husband and said: "What an unlucky creature I am! How I was cheated! I bought this for a good pot, and here it's got a hole in it! Look, husband!" So saying, she put it before his face and winked at the other to get out. And the husband said: "What a fool you are! The pot is perfect, perfect!" Then the woman gave the pot a slap and said: "Praise God! I thought it had a hole in it." And so the other got away.

I could give you a thousand examples of this, but I shall refrain for lack of space and because I do not wish to teach women who are already experts in wickedness. I shall be scolded by some for setting down these things, for they will say that I teach wickedness instead of correcting it; but they are ignorant of my purpose, which God knows is not evil in this matter. Let them say what they please, because I do not write to teach evil, but to inform men and women that, no matter how carefully they conceal their wickedness, it will be discovered; also that, armed with this knowledge, some will be able to correct their wives, daughters, and kinswomen, who, if they are wise and understanding, will abate their evil-doing in some degree. And let no man or woman think I pretend that what I write here has not been written a thousand times already by others, because there is nothing new under the sun. It may happen, however, that a man will be ignorant of these things and will read them here, and thus he will be able to correct those it is his duty to correct. Otherwise, if he fails to do so and puts up with it, let him not be astonished if disaster overtakes him. I say this with the best intention, and let him who reads take it in good part, for the love of God, and grumble not, for the world is so wicked today that good words are held in as much abhorrence as death itself, and evil words are pure delight. This by way of justifying myself, for I know well enough that as I have spoken, so shall I be spoken of, for many others have been treated in this fashion whose shoes I am unworthy to latch. Let God be my witness, in whose service I took it upon myself to say and write something in this matter.

CHAPTER ELEVEN

⌐ *How a man should be on his guard*
against a drunken woman

If a woman takes to bibbing wine you may be sure she will become a great drunkard, for there is no woman who takes pleasure in the drinking of wine who, if she visits fifty of her gossips, will not take a nip with each. Moreover, however much she has drunk already, if she is offered wine again, she will take another little sip just to see whether it has been properly cured. Water is poison to such and makes her burst into tears, for it rolls about in her stomach until she spews it up.

And now I will tell you what happens to her when she gets into the habit of drinking. First, from the third hour onward, when she begins to drink, what with the heat of the wine she drank the night before, she gets warm and her wits begin to wander, and she raises her eyes to heaven and sighs. Then she lowers her head and rests her chin upon her breast, and then she smiles and begins to chatter like a magpie and pick quarrels with everyone she meets. She bustles about, her eyes inflamed and rimmed with red, her speech thick. She talks through her nose and stumbles and threatens everyone, fierce as a lioness, for she has no respect for husband or master, but is out for trouble, and he is a wise man who ignores her until she has slept it off. Nor should a man strike her, or correct her, or scold her, for she is in no state to be taught, but will make a saucy answer and act dishonestly. Nor should he forbid her to drink wine. Nor will it do him any good to mix wormwood with it and make her drink it, or to cook eels in it, or put sulphur in it and boil out the alcohol, or to mix hemp water in it, or ergot dried in the sun and ground. Nor will it avail him to soak asafetida, a kind of gum, in it for two days and then strain and purify the wine and give it to her to drink. And the same with many other remedies for drunkenness.

On the other hand, there are women who will cheerfully take anything you give them to cure their appetite, and these put great faith in such remedies, but they do not put their faith in the remedy of remedies, nor will they use it, that is, their good sense and natural understanding which, if they would only obey its counsel, would forever stop their drinking and is the best of all cures. A curse on a woman (and a man too, for that matter) who sees that she loses her wits when she drinks, and that when she is drunk she is made a butt of, and

everyone laughs at her and jeers at her, however
high her estate, her own people as well as strangers,
her kinsmen, her husband, her children! For the
same reason she is beaten, whipped, and buffeted,
and no one trusts her. Her house is bare of money,
jewels, and silver, of everything of value, of fine
clothes to wear and display at parties, weddings, and
merrymakings, and where she might be mistress and
command, she is a slave and a captive, spurned and
mocked and jeered at by all who see her! Oh, luckless wretch, foolish and ignorant, unwise and of
little understanding!

Tell me now, the most beautiful woman you
know, as soon as she gives herself up to this vile
habit of drinking and is well drunken, be she wife,
nun, servant, widow, spinster, or mistress, hot with
wine and addled in her wits, would she deny her
body to anyone who wanted it? Certainly not! For
she is beside herself and out of her mind; nor is she
in any condition to consider her honor or dishonor.
Many of them become thieves, stealing in order to
drink, hiding bottles and jugs about the house, under
the bed, under their clothing, and even in their
chests, so as to be able to fill their skins with wine.
A curse on her who knows this weakness in herself
and does not fly from wine wherever she sees it!
If a woman is a drunkard, however comely, however high her estate, however beautiful she may be,
she is held to be lower than the lowest beast. Be sure
of this: that such a woman cannot avoid being a
thief, a wanton with her body, filthy, mad, a chatterbox. Do not look for fear, dread, or shame in
her. Fly her company as from a mortal enemy. And
if, for your sins, you must live with her, strive to

get along with her as well as you can, and, if it is not possible for you to abandon her, she being your wife, mother, or daughter, or one you cannot abandon, and you have to put up with her, prepare your winding sheet before you attempt to reform her or cure her of her sickness, for with her lack of sense she is a bad one to check. What else can you expect if her wits have gone wandering?

There are still others who do not get drunk in this way but who are warmed with wine. These you will find very gay while they are in wine and very playful, and at that moment they are disposed, given the place and the opportunity, to commit every wickedness. They will promise you more and give you more in one hour at such a time than in twenty hours at any other. Then it is that they will argue, scold, and grumble with their own people, but show themselves affable to strangers. Although such women may not be evil, yet they bring down many evils upon themselves from their drinking, and upon their households, their affairs, and estates, because they babble foolishly while in drink. So many are these evils, indeed, that it is better not to mention them, lest I instruct those who are inclined to evil-doing and prevent their correction when they are bent on mischief.

Moreover, as I have said already, she who drinks immoderately has a stinking breath, her hands tremble, her senses are dulled, she sleeps little and eats less, and her whole life is given up to drinking and endless scolding. These and other things are the result of it. Therefore, a woman who drinks immoderately is properly called a drunkard and is considered to be such by the people, and is not fit to appear in public. And she who talks too much about wine deserves to be set in a corner and soundly slapped by her husband.

CHAPTER TWELVE

↰ *How a chattering woman always talks about the affairs of others*

It is a general rule that women are chatterboxes, for there is not a woman alive who does not want to be always talking and listened to. It is not her custom to give another the opportunity to speak in her presence, and if the day lasted a year she would never tire of talking day or night. Thus you will see that many women are so in the habit of talking that they talk to themselves when there is no one else to talk to. You will also see that, with her talking and evil-speaking, a woman can stop the mouths of ten men. When they cannot convince you by reasoning, off they go into railing, and that is why they can never keep a secret from anyone. I say that you should beware, as you would avoid a fire, of having words with a woman who knows some secret of yours, for, as I have said, an angry woman cares not what she says, whether the secret be deadly or venial, and what you most urgently beg her to keep secret, that is what she will be bursting to tell and make public. So true is this that you will find women everywhere in holes and corners and out-of-the-way places, talking about their neighbors and friends and their goings-on, and especially about other people's affairs. They are always gabbling and poking their noses into other people's business: how

So-and-so lives, how much money she has, how she dresses, what kind of match she made, how her husband hates her and how she deserves it, and what was said about her at church. And others will answer in kind, and so they waste their time in folly and in things vain beyond description. Hence, it is a universal rule that wherever women are, there will be a lot of babbling.

The blessed creatures gather in flocks, many of them matrons, others girls of one age or another, and they begin and never end, talking about other people's daughters, or about newcomers—in the winter round the fire, in the summer in the open, two or three hours on end, saying: "So-and-so, the wife of What's-his-name and the daughter of What-you-may-call-her, upon my word, you'd hardly know her! What a little sheep of St. Blas! What a lambkin of St. Anthony! I wouldn't trust her!" Etc. And another will answer: "Oho, and if you only knew what a wicked tongue she has! Lord, Lord! And how modestly she acts, for God's sake! Do you follow me, my friend? Anyone seeing her so innocent. . . ." Etc. Thus they spend all their time in corners backbiting.

And if you want to learn some odd things about women, go to the bake oven or a wedding, or to church, where you will never see them but they are whispering in each other's ears, or laughing at each other, some taking up with the enemies of others, primping and flaunting their finery and strutting—this to outshine them—although they know that they themselves would sell their bodies for jewels and gimcracks, and they say: "Well, burn me if I don't put your nose out of joint next

Sunday!" And the winsome wenches of one neighborhood will plot against the gallant girls of the next and say: "Let's see now who can get herself the more gaped at and talked about! Do they think they can put on a better show than we can? We can beat them, and let's see what they will do about it! Oho, my friend, and don't you see how they are eying us? Let's run them off and bark at them! Let's laugh and whisper and look at them, and you'll see how red they get! Or, before they get up let's walk in front of them so their admirers will bow to us instead of to them. Let's try that for a start, and see how they like it!"

These and an infinite number of other things, too many to be described, women work at and plot, talking and gossiping about other people's affairs. Hence we may conclude that woman is a chatterbox and a bad keeper of secrets, and that he who does not trust them has a treasure beyond price, and that he who avoids their goings-on and ignores them will live in greater peace—this I assure him.

CHAPTER THIRTEEN

How women love any man they please, of whatever age

There is no rule that says a woman shall love a man unselfishly and truly; nor does experience prove or doctrine teach it; nor is there any woman who does so, however much you may seek to love her and be loved by her, for this, as I have said, would be like trying to move a mountain against the course of nature. But as for being loved herself, that is a different matter, especially if she sees she is not beautiful or handsome, and lacks the graces and qualities that attract the love of men, for men do not love the beautiful alone, but the gracious, the pleasant-spoken, the witty, honest, clean, courteous and well-mannered, of honest habits always, and modest. These are the ones who deserve to be loved, even though they may not be as beautiful or as comely as others, for many are beautiful, fair, blonde, of marvelous features, but are in themselves so base, vile, filthy, and covered with blemishes, and of such evil ways, that they think their beauty alone will suffice to attract the love of men.

I well believe that he who does not know such may fall in love with one at first sight, but that when he really knows her he will fly her company and love her no more, as soon as he has had his pleasure of her. Then he turns her out and will not see her again until his unbridled lust makes him seek her. The worst of it is, and this is a great sin, that when a woman sees that a man's love for her is cooling, or even if it is not, she begins to cast what she calls love spells and charms, more truly called diabolical witchcraft. This she does, sometimes to attract the love of others who love her less, sometimes to fan the love of him who already loves her, to prevent his thinking another woman more comely, and to make him cast aside all others and abhor God and the world for her. This is the work of certain old crones, accursed of God and His saints and enemies of the Virgin Mary. These are women who have destroyed and dishonored themselves and condemned themselves to perpetual torment by persevering in their enormous sins. And, when they can

no longer practice their trade and are now so old
that they are hated and unloved, then it is that they
turn to procuring, spellbinding, and soothsaying, to
bring about the ruin of others like them. O accursed,
excommunicated, infamous, treacherous, malevolent
women, deserving to be burned alive! How many
pregnant women have you aborted because they
were shamed in the eyes of the world: matrons,
widows, nuns, and even the betrothed! Oh, if I
only dared write what I have heard, seen, and
learned in this matter! But it would only make me
enemies for the sake of telling the truth, or, at
worst, instruct the innocent and make it possible for
them to do evil in the hope of escaping the consequences. Hence, my pen ceases.

And yet, tell me, these false old gulls, how many
do they kill or drive mad with their accursed love
charms? How many quarrels are they the cause of
between husbands and wives, and how many dark
deeds do they do with their spells and curses? They
cause husbands to abandon their wives and run off
with strange women; the same with wives, to leave
their husbands and take up with others. They bring
about the downfall of the daughters of good men,
and not a maid or a widow or a matron but is
driven mad by their witchcraft. And still the stupid
fools hurry off to these old hags and their charms
as if they were running for an indulgence.

In Barcelona I knew one such whose house was
always full of this nonsense, an old hag of seventy.
I saw her hanged from the balcony of a man she had
murdered by applying poison to his armpits; and
they also hanged her by the neck at the door of a
matron that she had killed, and burned her later for

a witch at Caned, outside the city; nor was she saved by the great favor she enjoyed with many gentlemen. This sin is now so common and tolerated that the people pay no attention to it. You should, therefore, take this lesson to heart, and others like it.

Tell me now, what is the fate of a woman who abandons a rich and noble husband, except an evil old age and a bad end? I say that such a woman, whose duty it is to love, cherish, and honor her husband, gets herself involved at times, as you will see, in a wicked affair with some poor and paltry wretch, dishonoring herself as well as her husband. Can such a woman really love her husband? Certainly not! For if she loved him she would not dishonor him. This is what comes of the small love a wife has for her husband: she loves him only so long as he submits to her and does her bidding, for I say unto you that, however much a wife appears to love her husband, even though he does her a thousand favors, let him do one thing she does not like and then you will see strife in his house, and tears and scowls and black looks, and she will turn her back on him. She will refuse to eat or drink, so furious is she, that is, while he is present, for after he goes out she will eat aplenty. Moreover, she will not sit at the table with him or go to bed with him, but will sleep on a bench, making a show of weeping and sobbing. And she will get up during the night and curse her fate, and look so sad that there is not a husband in the world who will not cover his wife with kisses at that moment. And then, when she has got her way, the next morning the house is full of laughter and she is happy as a bird. "Take this to my husband," she says, and she embraces and kisses him, and combs his hair and does him all manner of kindnesses.

See, then, how much a wife loves her husband and cherishes him, and the good will she has for him, for the poor wretch is the one who had to yield and make friends with her. And if a wife treats her husband in this fashion, what can some other wretch expect of a woman who, once she is beyond his threshold, makes fun of him for a coward, and in his presence winks and makes a mouth at her neighbor, tripping him up to make a fool of him. It is folly, therefore, to trust a woman, idiocy to love one, and nonsense to suffer for one. So on your way, my friend! A woman must know that there is nothing more irritating to her husband or lover than for her to yield her body to another. You may well ask whether she loves him or wishes deliberately to vex him when she commits such an act against the one she says she loves, at times giving her body to a stranger or a pilgrim, unknown to anyone, merely to satisfy with him her unbridled lust.

Hence you should know that a woman will frequently dissemble her lack of love, lack of desire, and lack of goods. Think well, my friend, what a fox's broth a woman is, for she seems cold but she burns; inwardly she is on fire with love, but she conceals it, because if she revealed it she thinks she would be despised. Therefore, she would be begged in all things, giving you to understand that what she does, she does against her will, and she says: "Oh, go away! I won't do it! Oh, what a stubborn brute! By my faith, I'll leave you! By God, I'll scream! Be quiet now! For God's sake don't be a nuisance! Stop it now! Don't be rude! Have you no shame? Are you in your right mind? Behave yourself now, somebody's looking! Don't you see? Stop it now, you beast! By my faith I'll get angry! I'm not joking! Will you stop? Do you want me to tell you a thing or two? God deliver me from this devil! Get out! What a clod you are! What a bore! Woe is me! Ouch, you've broken my finger! Ouch, you're hurting my hand! The devil brought this fellow here, poor wretch that I am, poor luckless wretch, born in an evil hour! It was a black moment for me when I came to this house! May you die in agony! May you die of the rabies, you devil, you damned nighthawk! Does he think I am as strong as he is? He's broken every bone in my body! He's crushed both my hands! Oh, Lord! By God, you'll never come here again! Let this be a lesson to me! The devil must have brought me here! A curse on my life! I wish I were dead, poor wretch! Who lied to me? A curse on her who ever trusts a man, amen!"

These and other things women say to save their faces, but God knows what is in their hearts, or how hard they try to run away or resist. They scream aplenty, but stay where they are. They wave their arms, but do not move their bodies. They whine, but do not stir. They make a great show of resisting and let on that they are in pain and agony. Of women, therefore, believe only what you see, and of what you see, the half or less. And do not believe in their love, for it is vain and fickle, transitory and not lasting, as I have said; it lasts only so long as they please. This is the substance of it, and let us have no further argument, but remember that when you think you have got something from them you have nothing.

CHAPTER FOURTEEN

How the only wisdom is to love God, and all else is folly

So, my friend, bear in mind that the only wisdom consists in loving God, virtue, and valor. Infinite good is in store for him who loves God from his heart, for the love of worldly things, riches, women, and station is a vain and foolish love, and a vice contrary to all virtue, and from it come many evils, as I have said. If you will consider, moreover, what a thing the woman is whom you love, and what virtues she has, what character, what constancy, and what it is that you are dying for and losing your soul over, be sure that your heart will never be set upon anything but God, for all things pass except His love. It is a good thing, my friend, for a man to risk ruin or death in a good cause, but for him to die and ruin himself for a base and transitory thing shows little sense and a lack of natural judgment. Therefore, my friend, let us so conduct ourselves that we shall be loved by that true Sidrach,[11] Jesus Christ, son of our humble and gracious advocate, the Holy Virgin Mary, not, indeed, because we deserve it, but because He shed His blood for us of His own free will on the tree of the Holy Cross, to redeem us from the sin to which our Father Adam and our Mother Eve condemned us. If a man should contemplate this true love and ponder it awhile, I verily believe that it would be impossible for him greatly to err.

Now that I have dwelt somewhat upon the wickedness of women, it is fitting for me to shift the

direction of my words and propositions, lest it be
said of me that all I am doing is to speak ill of
women and not of the wicked men who for our
infinite sins are to be found in this world. Some men
do wickedly, persevere in it, and come to a bad end.
Others, on the contrary, do wickedly, persevere in
it, and come to a very good end. Still others do
good, persevere in it, and end very badly. I shall,
therefore, treat of them at some length, protesting
that I shall say nothing bad of a good man, which
would be wicked and against my conscience, and
improper besides. Neither do I wish to condemn
others merely to clear myself; rather, I confess my
guilt and wish to be counted among the erring sinners I shall describe. It may so happen that a man
who is himself wicked will serve as an example for
the correction of others, as I have said, and that is
what I should like to do, God willing, because many
of us are like a torch which destroys itself while
giving light. May it so please Almighty God, who
gives His gifts to whom He pleases and as He
pleases, to vouchsafe me His grace in this little book
of mine, and in others which in His service and
praise I, unworthy, intend to write, so that someone
will learn good from it, and by his mending, instruction, and correction redeem the sins I have committed; for Our Lord often distributes His graces
where He pleases and how He pleases, because to
each of us He gives as much as He wills, and even
more, because where the spirit of God wishes to
inspire, there it inspires. As Our Lord says in His
Holy Gospel: "Lord, many secret things didst Thou
conceal from the wise and prudent which Thou
didst reveal unto the humble, as was Thy will." In

conclusion, many great men of letters, the saints and God's chosen, were of the same opinion, especially St. Augustine, who said: "We see in the world certain men of violence who are hated by mankind and held in small esteem by the simple, the poor, the ignorant, and the weak, and who rob and ravish heaven itself with force, fury, and violence, and there is no moderation in them. And we, with all our wisdom and learning, are cast into the abyss!"

I do not make this comparison because I am one of the wise or one of the violent, for I know well enough that I am merely one of the ignorant who hope for God's compassion; and I say this without self-adulation because I know it to be the truth. And yet, the simple can give good counsel to others, even though they cannot take it themselves, and sometimes a man can reprehend who is more to be reprehended than any other. The good man gives little attention to the wicked or his evil ways; nor does he who would learn care whether his teacher is himself wicked and of evil works. Let him heed the words of his teacher and profit by them and give no heed to his works, for the teacher will have to answer for them. Each of us must bear his own burden and make an accounting at his strict trial, for the son may not take upon himself the sins of the father, nor the father those of the son. On the other hand, I say that he is worthy of the highest praise who teaches by deed as well as by word, and that God is within him. But who is this man whom we praise? He is one who works miracles in his life, for the rest of us, some more, some less, are sinners, and if we say we have not sinned we deceive ourselves, as St. John says in the first chapter of his

Epistle, that there is no man who has lived without sin. Therefore, I count myself among their number and say that I am the chief sinner among those about whom I shall speak. If I speak well, let me not be reprehended, and if I speak ill, I wish to be corrected, not only by the learned, but by anyone who thinks I err in my teaching, writing, or speaking.

Since the purpose of this book is the reprobation of worldly love and praise of the love of God, and since up to this point I have reproved the love of women, it would not be fitting for me to praise the love of men. If women wish to love men, let them consider who it is they love, what profit there is in it, and what virtues and vices men have for loving. And, since men are not commonly reproved in this as women are—this because of their greater sense and judgment—it will be fitting, then, to speak of each man according to his nature, which cannot be known without the natural science of the astrologers. It will be necessary, therefore, first to know the planets and signs, what and how many they are, how they influence inferior bodies, what the several complexions of men are, how each can be recognized, and how women can protect themselves from men. And if, perhaps, it should be said that this does not concern the reprobation of love, I say it does, very much indeed, no less than what I said about the love of women. Generally speaking, however, the complexions of women are different from those of men, and women take pleasure in willfully acting according to them, as I have said. And now I beseech the reader not to be impatient with me for failing to cite more authorities. My reasons are two: first, examples of vice and virtue taken from experience are more effective, although they may sound like old wives' tales or ballads, and even though some scholars will say they are nothing but gossip and not fit for the public. Let them forgive me and take it in good part, for what else could I do but show how the world lives, since in the examples themselves the great vices are reproved? My second reason is that how can he, who neither knows nor understands the authorities, speak with authority? This is the sum of all the arguments made against me in this part.

⌐ PART THREE

Here begins the third part of this book which will treat of the complexions of men and the planets and signs, what they are and how many they are.

CHAPTER ONE

↱ Of the complexions

Of men there are many kinds, and hence they are hard to know and harder to teach. The heart of a man is a very deep thing, as Solomon says, but it can be known, not only by its outward manifestations, but by the qualities and complexions that each one possesses, by which he is held to be good or bad. There are four principal kinds of men, divided according to their qualities. Some are secretive, silent, of few words, phlegmatic, and sour-tempered. There are three other classes. One is sanguine, happy and pleasure-loving; another, choleric and furious; the third, melancholy, sad, and gloomy. All this, however, is relative, because each man is composed of all four complexions, but one of them will predominate above the others, as I shall explain later on. I shall speak first of the better complexions according to their degree of excellence, and according to their nature and the influence of their planets, for it is certain that the celestial bodies exert an influence upon inferior bodies and modify them, some more, some less.

CHAPTER TWO

↰ Of the sanguine man

First, I say that certain men are sanguine, with a very small admixture of some other quality or complexion, but not greatly dominated by any other. These fellows correspond to the element of air, which is humid and hot. They are joyous, easily pleased, full of laughter, playful and bright, dancers, light of limb, openhanded, fat, fond of every pleasure, and enemies of all disagreeableness. They laugh heartily and are delighted with every joyful and well-done thing. Their face is fresh, their color high and beautiful; they are bold, honest, and moderate. They are merciful and just, for they love justice, but will not do it by their own hands or be the instrument of its execution. Rather, they are so tenderhearted that they will not watch the death of any living thing and are filled with pity for any brute beast they see sick or dying. They are pained by evil-doing, for they love to do good and see it done. In sum, the sanguine man, if he is free of an excess of some other quality, is called fortunate. He is under the influence of these three signs: Gemini, Libra, and Aquarius, whose kingdom is in the west.

CHAPTER THREE

↰ Of the choleric man

Other men are choleric. They are hot and dry, corresponding to the element of fire. These fellows are hotheaded and have no moderation whatever. They are very proud, strong, and of a hasty temper, which, to be sure, lasts only a short time, but while it lasts they are exceedingly violent. They are ready of speech, daring in every situation, courageous, agile of body, learned, subtle, and witty, and very eager and active. They abhor all laziness and are fitted for great deeds. They love justice. They are not as good at commanding as they are at executing, and thus they are like cruel butchers when they are filled with wrath, but repentant once it has passed. Their color is pale. They are under the influence of these three signs: Aries, Leo, and Sagittarius, whose kingdom is in the east. Such men often cause the ruin of others.

CHAPTER FOUR

⌐ *Of the phlegmatic man*

Other men are phlegmatic: humid, cold, of the nature of water. These fellows are tepid, neither good enough for this world, nor bad enough for the next; rather, they are lazy and negligent. It is all the same to them whether a thing comes or goes. They are sleepy, heavy, and duller than clods. They are good for neither laughter nor tears. They are cold, wintry, of few words, solitary, ill-formed, half dumb, suspicious, and keep to themselves. They are weak-witted and stupid, cowardly in thought and even more in deed. They are under the influence of Cancer, Scorpio, and Pisces, whose kingdom is in the north. Their color is dropsical.

CHAPTER FIVE

↱ *Of the melancholy man*

Still other men are melancholy, and these correspond to earth, the fourth element, which is cold and dry. These fellows are very wrathful, unrestrained beyond measure, superlatively closefisted, insufferable wherever they happen to be, very quarrelsome and ready to pick a fight with anyone. They are intemperate in all their actions and dash their heads against the wall. They are very wicked, evil-spoken, gloomy, and given to sighing and sad thoughts. They avoid every resort of pleasure and dislike to see a man amusing himself with trifles. They are ugly-tempered and quickly come to blows. They are disputatious, lying, and deceitful, and have innumerable other defects and blemishes. They are rotten; they hawk and spit and scowl, and are excessively cruel in their actions.

The melancholy man is under the influence of Taurus, Virgo, and Capricorn, whose kingdom is in the south. His color is yellowish.

What I have said above is to be understood of those who are predominantly under the influence of one of the said humors, but if another and better humor should dilute the bad one and be present in greater strength, it will cause a man to lose his own complexion and lean toward the other, changing him in the direction of the better, and vice versa. For example, a phlegmatic man may be so helped in his blood that he will become something much better than phlegmatic, or he may be changed for the worse, and this applies to all the other complexions. But, as I have said, a man is composed of all four and the one that predominates is the one that determines his nature to a greater or lesser degree, each according to its domain.

CHAPTER SIX

↱ *How the signs influence the parts of the body*

You have heard now what the four complexions of man are (and what I have told you about man applies equally to women): sanguine, choleric, phlegmatic, and melancholy. Each body is made up of all these four complexions and none is without any, but the most influential is the one that determines a man's principal complexion and thus is known, in the body where it has its being, as the queen of the others. Moreover, men have the four elements that correspond to the four complexions: fire to the choleric man, water to the phlegmatic man, air to the sanguine man, earth to the melancholy man. Besides, three of the twelve signs predominate in each element or complexion: Aries, Leo, and Sagittarius in the choleric man, corresponding to the element of fire; Cancer, Scorpio, and Pisces in the phlegmatic man, corresponding to the element of water; Gemini, Libra, and Aquarius in the sanguine man, corresponding to the element of air; Taurus, Virgo, and Capricorn in the melancholy man, corresponding to the element of earth. So much for the complexions of the human body.

Item: Aries is masculine and influences the head; its planet is Mercury. Taurus is feminine and influences the body; its planet is Venus. Cancer is feminine and influences the breast; its planet is the moon. Leo is masculine and influences the heart; its planet is the sun. Virgo is feminine and influences the bowels and stomach; its planet is Mercury. Libra is masculine and influences the navel; its planet is Venus. Scorpio is feminine and influences the privy parts; its planet is Mars. Sagittarius is masculine and influences the thighs and spine; its planet is Jupiter. Capricorn is feminine and influences the knees; its planet is Saturn. Pisces is feminine and influences the feet; its planet is Jupiter. So now you know all the twelve signs, six feminine and six masculine, as I said above.

To get back to my argument—we still have to speak of the natural marks borne by different people, indicating what their nature is, that is: curly-haired or red-haired or prematurely gray; round- or long-headed; brows wrinkled or with cowlicks or hair growing very low on them; eyebrows meeting; flat noses, *canusos*,[12] or great long noses, or thin and sharp noses; deep-set eyes, small, with scanty lashes, or red, or spotted; large mouth; lisping or stuttering speech; teeth sharp and uneven; cleft chin; face wide and round; large dangling ears; heavy protruding jaw; prematurely bearded; neck short and thick; one-eyed or cross-eyed or squinting in both eyes; lame or stoop-shouldered or humpbacked, single or double; the body covered with hair, or hairless and smooth; wide hips; crooked legs; malformed hands and feet; soft- or hasty-spoken; demeanor calm or excitable; lying; haughty, and so many other characteristics that it would take a great while to tell you what each one signifies.

You will find the matter treated at length in the book called *De secretis secretorum,* which Aristotle wrote for Alexander, near the end of it. There you will read wonderful things about the attributes of persons, and how at times they will lie because of their great judgment, when they are ruled by it. But, since this rule is not found to be continuous or true, I will not pursue the subject further, lest they who read this should quarrel with one another, saying: "You have such a mark, I have this one, and What's-his-name that one, so it follows that he is this kind of person and you are that." Therefore, I will drop it, especially since there are some men who have a high color and are good men in spite of it, and so on with the other marks. Those who bear them should be sensible and discreet enough to avoid error and the characteristic which their mark indicates for them, and will be able to conceal their defects wisely. Leaving all this to one side, therefore, let us get on to our intent and conclusion.

CHAPTER SEVEN

Of the attributes of the sanguine man

I will now speak to you of the attributes of men and women, although we are not concerned here with women, because I have said a bit about them already, such a small bit, however, that it does not amount to a grain of millet in an ass's mouth for their instruction and correction, but enough for him who wishes, to take advantage of it, or has the ability to do so. I have spoken so little of the vices and faults of men that I was like a cat walking on hot coals, so now I shall speak of them at greater length, of my own as well as those of other men, taking their complexions as my starting point, what they are, how they work, and what influences they have. And first I shall speak of the sanguine man: what blemishes he has, what evils and vices, and what virtues and good qualities.

Well, then, first of all, the sanguine man is very gay, open, laughing, and pleasure-loving; but, although the sanguine man naturally has these good qualities, if he uses them badly he corrupts and transforms them into bad ones, for, since he is gay and pleasure-loving, he is very lecherous and his heart burns like fire, and he loves to left and to right. Every woman he sees he loves and desires, and with all of them he is very gay, justifying himself by what the prophet David says in his Psalm: *"For Thou, O Lord, hast made me glad through Thy work.* Therefore, O Lord, if I love, I love and desire the woman who is beautiful, for she is the work of Thy hands, and, since the prophet so commands, O Lord, I should not be sinning."

My friend, my answer is that this pleasure is for the worship of God, not for sinning. You may take pleasure in woman, and you will not sin, if you say: "All praise to Thee who created such a beautiful thing!" If this is your pleasure it is good, not only with respect to women, but to all things God created. If, on the other hand, seeing her beauty you desire her in order to sin with her, this is not a delight but a sin, and the prophet did not have this in mind. Others say: "How is it that God created man and woman with carnal appetites, but forbade them to indulge in them?" This proposition you will find reproved by the pope in the last *Clementina, De haereticis,* in the seventh error of the German Beghards, where the pope defines copulation as a mortal sin, except with one's wife, and even then it is not always free of mortal sin. The Beghards held that the act of copulation was not a mortal sin, because we are naturally inclined to it, especially since we are strongly tempted by its Author to commit it—a proposition refuted by all the Doctors of the Church. I say that God made us so in order to multiply the species by copulation, in matrimony, and He gave us this urge so that those who should resist it might be rewarded, for a reward cannot be had without effort. Therefore, let him who would achieve glory and everlasting joy suffer a bit for God and His love, although He, because of your suffering, has no more and no less pain than He has had since the beginning of time. What He desires is a good heart and a good will, and not mad love, either of women or of men.

A woman is pleased with gay, loving, and fascinating men, but only on condition that they love none but her, for that is the purpose for which a woman is born into the world and for which her mother raised her. But a woman in her folly does not understand the sanguine man and takes up with him, and he, with his pleasantries, festivals, jests, and games, deceives many women, and mocks and ruins them. Woe to the wretched woman who trusts him, for his love is spread among many and he is loved by many! He cannot be constant in love—let the stream flow under the bridge as long as the water lasts! Sanguine men are great jesters and mockers of the world: here today, gone tomorrow; if I don't like Marina, I'll try Catalina. Their sole purpose is to be gay, laughing, openhanded, and pleasure-loving; to have beautiful faces and bodies; to be players and singers; to be gay dogs in all their actions; so with the vainglory of their noble reputation they go quite mad. It is not in their power to love one woman alone, because they are loved by many. So the woman who takes him for herself or who, out of pure envy, takes him from another, considers herself superior, for there is nothing in which a woman will take more pride than in getting a husband or lover of such quality, even though she loses her good name among the people and is vituperated by her kinfolk.

Woe to the mad and wretched woman who is faithful to any man, for there are many men who, when tempted by another woman, cannot refuse! Thus many women are ruined and come to a bad end and lose the chance of a good marriage, as well as their honor and estate, because they trusted a man who, once he has had his will with her, has no more regard for her than for a thing forgotten. A woman will believe him when he promises and swears: "I'll give you this; I'll do that for you; I'll work wonders!" And even while he is swearing he is saying in his heart: "If she believes me, oh, how I'll fool her!" And if she does believe him, she will suffer doubly for it as long as she lives, for he has been paid in advance and will dishonor her and fail to keep his word, but will go to another woman to frolic and leave her out in the cold. This he will do, even though he has taken her away from her own country and brought her to a foreign land, or has taken her from her husband's house, or from that of her parents, or from the protection of her cousin or brother; and even though she is pregnant he will not honor his oath or promise. Therefore I say unto you that if any woman should suffer as much hardship in the service of God, or hunger and thirst, cold and travail, or even the half of it, as she suffers in running off with such a man, following him and believing his lies, bearing children for him and raising them, and spending bad nights and days and evil hours with him, she would go straight as an arrow to the glory of Paradise with no delay whatever!

Who can imagine all the ills, perils, and hardships to which a woman exposes herself after she has erred? Or even during the time she is erring? All the insults she must face, with death at her very elbow? But she has no thought but to close the door after her and be on her way, and long live folly! Certain it is that she would not put up with such a life with her husband, father, or kinfolk; rather, she would cut her throat first! And to get out from under the authority of her father and mother, husband or kinfolk, she will believe him who will not only command her, but will drive her like a donkey: "Get up, there! Whoa, there!" And then, when his love has cooled—at most it will last a year, if it lasts that long—from that moment onward she will travel with a cudgel at her back, and all this for love of a man who never misses a wink of sleep or a meal for her! Suffice it to say that she had already lost him when he captured and betrayed her, and she carelessly lost a husband, marriage, and honor because of him; and then his love evaporated when he had had his pleasure of her. But she, who began by loving him tepidly, by continual practice found her love burning as hot as a fire in tow, and as it increased she lost her desire for food and drink, sleep, and enjoyment—very different from the earlier situation, in which he got hotter and hotter the more he pursued her, and she got cooler and cooler.

These sanguine fellows are very gay, pleasure-loving, and fond of laughter. They will laugh until they weep at a little bird in flight, quite unaffectedly. All such happy men are given to love. They take pleasure in all gaiety, especially in singing, playing, dancing, riming, and writing love letters. They are witty in speech, jovial in company, faithful to their promises, a party to every deed of valor. This is owing to their upbringing, for the rustic, reared outside the city, even though he is of the same complexion, cannot, because of his lack of gentle upbringing, be a courtier. Still, his complexion makes him ready for every kind of hospitality and kindness, save that in love he strains at the bit like an unbroken colt.

Therefore, let her who will believe me love only God, and let her love Him all her short life, which lasts but a day, and not waste it in folly, for she must account to Him for it, even for every idle word she speaks. Let her love her honor and good name. Let her love her kinfolk where it is proper to do so. Let her love herself rather than a man, and not lightly believe him or turn her eyes at the sound of the tambourine. Let her be content with her honesty, her renown and good name, eating herbs with bread and water, within her four walls, for this is worth more to her than a thousand puffings and follies and pomps and vainglories, in which she will suffer vituperation and scorn, foolishly loving. And let her

not believe a mad lover, however good a dancer he
may be, however handsome, however well he sings,
for all such are mockers save in honest matrimony.

CHAPTER EIGHT

*Of the choleric man: what qualities he
has for loving and being loved*

There is another kind of men who are not of such
pleasant traits as those I have just described. These
are the choleric men, in whom anger predominates
over their other humors. These fellows are very
curious and intelligent, ardent, keen, learned, and
witty, but they are easily aroused and very ready
with their hands. You will find that men who have
such traits are often so hasty in their actions that,
although they show their good qualities in one
direction, spoil them in another. In their loving
they do much harm, because, for one thing, they are
easily moved, fly instantly into a rage, and their
hands are always ready to strike. These are the spill-
ers of blood, for few are the quarrels they get into
in which they do not spill it. Women love such men,
therefore, frequently to avenge insults—when, for
example, someone calls them something less than
ladies, for such they hold themselves to be.

If anyone should speak a word to such a woman
which is not to her liking, or is somewhat disparag-
ing, and she hears that her choleric lover is coming,
her heart bursts with tears and sobs. And when he
enters she hides herself and pretends to do so because she is annoyed with him. And when he comes
in he says to her servants: "Where is What's-her-

name?" Or "Where is your mistress?" "Sir, she is
in the house, very sad and tearful." So he goes in to
her and she begins to wipe her eyes, even smearing
them with saliva to make it appear she has been
weeping, and rubs them a bit with her hands to
make them red and inflamed. And when he comes
in she hides her face in her arms, or turns it to the
wall. And he says at once: "What's the matter, my
dear?" And she replies: "Nothing." "Tell me, lady,
for God's sake, why are you crying?" And she
says: "For no reason at all." "Well then, what's this
all about?" "Upon my word, I tell you, nothing!"
"Damn it all, mistress, tell me what's going on!
Who has offended you? Why those tears? Tell me,
blast you!" Then she says: "I'm crying over my
hard fate."

At this she bursts into tears and rubs her eyes
very hard, swallowing saliva more poisonous than
arsenic, and she says to him: "Do you think it's
right for What's-her-name or So-and-so to insult
me in public, calling me whore and concubine? She
called me a married whore and said such nasty
things about me that I wish I had died before I
became your mistress! Alas, poor wretch that I am!
Now I am dishonored and undone! And by whom?
By a vile whore, dirt under my feet! Or by a low
scoundrel, scum of the earth! Do you think I'll put
up with that? Rather, I'll forswear myself, by God
and my soul! I'll run off with a Moor from over the
sea, or with the basest footman in Castile! That's
all I've got to say!"

So then, this fellow, being choleric and easily
aroused, with no hesitation whatever seizes his
sword and bolts out the door, not stopping to find

out whether it is true or not, or making any further inquiry, but only on the word of an interested party, and he will give himself to the devil to destroy the man or woman who has insulted his ladylove. Let him who has any sense first consider the author of the story: whether she told it while in a good humor or a bad; whether she was irate or calm; whether the other woman is his friend or his enemy, or the friend of a friend or a neighbor; and he will hesitate before he loses a friend for an enemy, that is to say, his mistress. And if the other is his friend, he will hold his tongue and not stir up a row, but will say to her: "My dear, you are out of sorts. I haven't had anything to eat or drink. Let's put this off till later, because I'm not up to it now. Be patient and I'll look after it, but not today."

But this is not what the foolish fellow does in his folly, but off he rushes, and when she sees him pick up his sword and run out of the house, she begins to scream: "Oh, luckless wretch that I am, bird of ill omen, sad and miserable creature! Come back! Don't go!" At the same time she is dying to hear the yelps of the other when he beats her, or those of the man when her lover stabs him or kicks him or clubs him. Meanwhile, the husband or kinsman of the other woman runs out and the devil is to pay! The lover kills or gets killed, he cuts or gets cut, and the whole business is nothing but trouble for both sides. And when he is brought back to her house wounded or having wounded, the blessed promoter of it all scratches her arse (speaking with due reverence) and says: "Unhappy creature that I am, shamed and undone! O Lord, what will become of me now? Who cut your face? Who killed

you? Who struck you such a blow? Holy Virgin!
Dear Jesus, to Thee I commend him! Don't break
my heart! Woe is me! Bring me eggs! Bring me
lint! Bring me wine to make a compress! Juanilla,
run and get the barber! Run, you whore and daughter of a whore! Marica, go get me an old shirt; he's
bleeding to death! Dear Jesus! Holy Mary! Bring
me some water; I'm fainting! Alas! Pedro, my son,
run and tell his brother to come at once! Juan, go
tell his friend that there's been a fight, but don't tell
him he's wounded! Martin, go call my gossip! Call
my neighbor! Oh, what a calamity! What a terrible
thing! What a frightful piece of bad luck! Poor
wretch that I am, miserable creature! How sad and
weary! O Virgin Mary! Speak, my friend, for
God's sake! Are you hurt? Unlucky wretch that I
am, born in an evil hour!" Etc.

God help us! You see what questions she asks! She
sees him with his face slashed, or stabbed with a
dagger or lance, and she says: "What's the matter?
Are you hurt?" A wife or a mistress or any other
woman who with her wild tears brings disaster upon
her husband or lover (whom, perhaps, she wants to
get rid of), deserves to have her face slashed as his
was, as a token of her victory, or as a lesson to
other women who get men to do evil, avenging
their tears or fancied insults, for tears, you will
find, flow more readily from a woman's eyes than
water from a spring. Thus he will lose his estate
and come to a bad end rather than put up with an
insult that soon passes, or suffer an injury, or break
his heart a little. He will lose his possessions and live
in hiding and run away, abandoning his country and
his house, and will wander about in foreign parts,

making a living for magistrates, constables, and notaries, and all because of those accursed, damned, unlucky, poisonous, cruel, and monstrous tears! O Lord, would that I could weigh the tears of a woman, had I but the knowledge! Truly, a single tear of hers outweighs a hundredweight of lead or copper! A curse upon him, amen, who does not ponder this and who, when he sees a woman in tears, does not consider that they are merely an instrument of vengeance on the part of one who lacks discretion, sense, and understanding!

Good and honest women will shy away when men come to them, in order to avoid evil, especially, most especially, if such are choleric men and ready with their hands, in whom wrath is sudden, and who in a moment or an hour will do a thing for which they will spend a year or a lifetime repenting; or they meet with sudden death and go unshriven to hell, and she is left sad and luckless with her wish fulfilled, her insult avenged, and her grudge satisfied; but her pain is only beginning, for she should have remembered that silence is golden.

In the Preamble to the *Clementinae*, under the heading of Silence, it says: "Let the speaker be wise in his speech." Moreover, Ovid says: "There is nothing less harmful than silence, nor is there a greater plague than a loose tongue, for it leads to great error." Cato says that the first of all virtues is to hold one's tongue, and Socrates: "I have suffered from speaking, never from silence." The Archpriest of Hita says: "It is wisdom to keep a temperate silence and folly to talk too much."

The choleric man is hot in loving, foolhardy in action, unwise when he is angry, eager and skillful in executing, never afraid in action, and, although his understanding is never asleep, his hands are always awake. Therefore, he is a dangerous one to love or be loved, and women should fly his advances, for he is as fickle as the wind, or the dew which is gone in a brief moment, and they should love only Him who endureth, as His love endureth, forever, until they are better advised.

CHAPTER NINE

Of the melancholy man: how he is given to quarreling

Other men are melancholy. These fellows are as bad as the ones I have described, even worse, for they are ill-tempered, morose, glum, wicked, malicious, and quarrelsome. Let those who love consider whether men of such vices can love or be loved, for when one of them makes love he bursts forth at once in wrath and arrogance, saying: "By God's body, I deserve to have such and such a woman, who is as good as you are, or better!" They think they can win a woman by frightening her, and some of them succeed, threatening and bullying the poor creatures until they make them succumb. On the other hand, when they are in a fit of melancholy, they are sad and glum, and the only thing they think of is to get revenge. No companionship lasts with them; no woman can stand them. They roam about by night looking for a row. By day they are dicers, dangerous in a fight, obstreperous, enemies of justice, bulliers of the weak. They steal and rob and take their neighbor's goods by force. There is no wickedness they will not commit for money, nor is there a woman they will not betray for profit. She who takes such for a husband may be certain of an early death or a short life.

CHAPTER TEN

r⌐ *Of the phlegmatic man: his qualities for loving or being loved*

Other men there are who are phlegmatic, and these fellows in the art of loving are the cleverest and most skillful in the world! For one thing, they are lazy, and in the beginning of love very cowardly, worse than Jews. Note their second quality: they are too stupid, weak-witted, and hesitant, too suspicious and insensitive, to be loved, and they never take part in affairs of glory or honor. In the third place, with respect to loving and being loved, you will see that they are endowed with every quality that is inimical to love; for I would have you know that he who would love or be loved, in this modern world of today, must be quick, very strong of heart, constant, free from suspicion, brave, tender, witty, even-tempered, openhanded, courteous, liberal, daring, ardent, understanding, forward in arms and given to knightly deeds.

Well now, this poor, phlegmatic, base, and luckless wretch, with such a character as his, how can he love or be loved? If he is told he must venture forth by night to see his ladylove, or to suffer cold or mud or bad weather, what does he do? First, he stretches, then he yawns, and then he puts his head out the door to see whether it is raining or snowing.

Then he shrugs and says: "Shall I go? Shall I stay? Yes, I'll go. But then if I do, I may be seen; I may get wet; I may get muddy; I may meet the watch and he will take away my sword, or he may chase me through the streets. And if I stumble I may fall down and muddy my shiny boots. I won't stir out of the house without my galoshes! And, oh my goodness, suppose some dog bites me on the leg! Or suppose somebody stabs me! Or hits me on the head with a rock! Or, if they catch me in her house, suppose they cut off that which I hold most precious! Or suppose they catch me on the way and give me a beating! I don't know. . . . The devil take me! Upon my word, I won't go! I won't leave the house! One's foot is well off on one's leg! I'll go to bed. He who is content and seeks trouble, if trouble comes, let God help him!"

But if this fellow, carried away by much love, does go forth to the house of his ladylove and meets some person carrying canes or hides that make a noise, then, he being weak of spirit and cowardly, his heart shrinks to the size of an ant's and he runs headlong, and stumbles and falls, and gets up stunned, and flies and looks over his shoulder to see if he is being pursued, for he imagines that armed men are puffing at his very back to kill him, so he flies heaven and earth. And if by chance he reaches the house of his ladylove, he will not enter by a window, for his courage is not up to it; nor will he use a rope ladder or unhinge a door; nor will he scale a garden wall ten feet high. And even when she opens the door for him he goes in shaking, for he imagines he sees armed men in every corner. And if a cat moves he is worse than a woman and falls in a swoon, and she must bring him to with smelling salts. And she says: "Courage, friend! It was only the cat, my love!" And the poor Jew, sweating like a man in the stocks, his color gone, the whites of his eyes showing, his heart jumping out of his mouth, says: "Lady, I am dead! I thought I saw just now more than a hundred men, and by the noise they made they were all armed! Lady, I am dead! Open the door, my friend, and let me out! I'm in the cold sweat of death!" And he looks about him to see how he can escape.

And she says: "Lord, man, don't be afraid! It was the cat, my love, that ran when it saw you." Or "It was the ducks splashing in the pond." Or "It was the mule munching barley." Or "It was the hen that has the pip." Or "It was my mother sifting flour." Or "It was my old mistress coughing." Or "It was the bitch scratching fleas or growling. Stay, friend, and calm yourself, for you are as safe here as in your own house, no doubt about it." But he answers: "Alas, lady, I want to go home! I'm afraid to stay! My hair is standing on end! Jesus, there's something wrong here!"

So when she sees that he is trembling as if with the ague and is more dead than alive, and when she sees that even if he did stay she would have no man with her, but a woman, she says: "Well, I don't need any more women around here!" Whereupon she opens the door and lets him out, and the blessings she heaps upon his head I hope will come to all such: an abundance of curses, insults unnumbered, figs, snorts, and whistles like those of an ox driver, and she says: "May your mother enjoy you! May she who gave you birth never bear another, amen!

Oh, what a lover! Pfui! He'd be a fine one to hold a door against ten or a dozen men and scare them off, so fearful was he!"

Thus it is that these fellows are good neither for loving nor being loved, since they lack what love demands and what a woman wants. To love such, therefore, is the lees of kindness and the dregs of meanness, although, to be sure, there are some women who would just as soon be loved by a sluggard as by a passionate man, by a weak man as by a strong, by a eunuch as by a whole man, by a clod as by an expert, by a villain as by a gentleman, by a slow man as by a quick. There is only one florin, they say, and nothing else counts. But this is the truth: that a man with only one shirt to his back may be worth more than another with thousands of doubloons. But those days are gone now, for even a man of seventy, if he believes a woman's lies and flattery, will convince himself that there is not his equal in the world. She will be happy if he gives her finery to wear, even though he is ugly and graceless, filthy, fat, and sleepy, because, with the food and drink he gives her, she will never lack some footman to frolic with later on. Woe to him who foots the bill!

This applies to women as well as men, for at times a man will love a dirty, ugly old bag, good for nothing, provided only that she has money and position. He thinks that such a woman is different from the others, but God knows that sometimes a woman clad only in a smock is worth more than another covered with marten skins. These are the unions which, in wedlock or in concubinage, yield the misshapen loaves, the crooked horns, and loveless mar-

riages, that is, when an old woman is given to a
young man in love or marriage, or a young woman
to an old man, or an old man to an old woman.
What can these ancients, filthier than spiders, expect
but bad luck and jealousy, and quarreling and
scratching and strife? What a fine foundation for
love!

CHAPTER ELEVEN

Of *matrimony*

There are four kinds of marriages, three to be condemned and one to be praised. The first is when
a young man marries an old woman. This good
mother, with her wrinkled belly, what has she to
look forward to but that the young man will flaunt
one or two or more mistresses before her eyes each
day? And let the accursed old crone burst with
jealousy and die the death, or live in pain! Or, if
she complains, let her wear a black eye, suffer daily
beatings and a broken head, and go about in a perpetual poultice! This is what the good old lady may
expect who in her last days takes a young husband
or lover, thinking in her folly that he will be content with her corrugated hide, or that she, the pious
old hypocrite, the lecherous bag of bones, will have
children by him in her silly dotage! Well, let the
toothless old hag, with her infernal white locks,
make her bed and lie in it! Let the accursed old
dragon die and burst who seeks pleasure at the edge
of the grave! Let her take comfort in her evil se-
nility, her tanned old hide, her wrinkled belly, her
stinking mouth and rotten teeth! For a youth a

pretty girl, and burn the rancid hag! And for a pretty girl a handsome youth, and let the old bore burst!

I would have you know that this good old lady violates the purpose of matrimony, which took its name, according to Leon Ostiense, in his *Summa* under this title, from *mater* and *munus*, meaning the office of motherhood. Other authorities, as, for example, the *Sacramental*, in the paragraph entitled *What Is Matrimony?*, say that it derives from *mater* and *munire*, which is to say, to protect, for it protects the mother from infamy and fornication. Still others say it comes from *monos*, meaning one, because one is engendered from the bodies of two. St. Isidore, in his *Etymologiae*, says that matrimony derives from *matrona*, which means the mother of the born child. Well now, our said good old lady was not concerned with observing the purposes of matrimony, but took the counsel of some silly fool, just to give herself a wicked old age. And do you know why it is not called *patrimony* but *matrimony?* It is because of the great hardship, pain, and travail that a woman must endure before the agony of delivery, and during it and after it, when she raises her brat. Hence it is called *matrimony* after the mother, but the leathery old crone was not thinking of this at all. Let her, therefore, have her evil life and let it serve her as a farewell to this world!

The second manner of marriage or union to be condemned is when an old man marries a young girl or takes her as his mistress. What does the hawking and spitting old fool, heavy as lead, full of depravities, expect, save that the girl, vexed beyond endurance at being tied to such a plow ox, will find a youth with whom to frolic? And he will have to take it and keep his mouth shut, and consent, and see his house go to ruin day by day, helpless to prevent it. The first prayer of the girl, when she gets into bed with her ancient husband, is: "A curse on the parents who would give their daughter to such!" And she makes a couple of figs at him and lies down beside him sighing, but not for him. Or she says: "May he who made this marriage never make another! May God give him a bad end, bad days, and worse years, amen!" Etc. Then she blows out the light, lies down at his side, turns her back to him, and says: "May God give you an evil old age, you putrid old goat, accursed of God and His saints, bent and sluggish, dirty and spitting, you boring old villain, rough as shark skin, stiff as an ox, potbellied as a gander, gray, bald, and toothless! To think I've got you lying next to me, you ill-humored old devil, you corpse, you scarecrow, you cold pig, sweating in summer and shivering in winter! Woe to her who suffers such a fate! Alas for her who has such at her side each night! Woe is me, born in an evil hour! To think that this was in store for me, poor wretch! Another enjoys her youth, but this evil old age was saved for me, alas! But, by God's Passion, if He will let me live another day, I'll get even with him! Ha! Does he think that I will put up with such a life? Rather, I'll burn in the middle of yonder square, poor wretch! May he who captured me see himself a captive in the land of the Moors, and soon, amen! O Lord, how many men would lift up their hands in praise of Thee if they could sleep with me! Lord, Lord, why don't I burst? Here I am! Cold I

came to bed and cold I'll awaken! I was born in an
evil hour! The side on which I lay down is the side
from which I'll get up! No unluckier woman was
ever born! Oh that my husband were young, even
though a cobbler, poor and penniless, anything but
this old devil I've got! What good is his money to
me, poor creature? What good his great name, alas, if
in my best years I am alone and might as well be
sleeping with my godmother, as I used! Do you call
this living? The devil take her who would stand for
it! But from now on I'll square my account, for this
is not to be endured!"

All this she says to herself, and she turns toward
him and pretends to scratch his head, but makes
horns with her fingers. She pretends to pat his
cheek, but makes a fig in his eye. She puts her arms
around him, but turns her face away and crooks
her finger at him, saying: "Upon my word, that's
the way it bends, you false old villain, limp as a
piece of sheepskin or rawhide! Cover me with
mourning, Lord, for this old traitor gives me a
pain!"

There is still another kind of marriage to be condemned, although not so much as those I have mentioned, that is, when an old man marries an old
woman, for there will never be anything but scolding and quarreling on both sides. They are never
happy, what with him in pain and her in more, and
she says: "Oh, my uterus! Oh, my kidneys! Oh, my
head! Oh, my tooth! Oh, my breast! Oh, my eye!
Oh, my hip! Oh, my stomach! Oh, my side! Oh,
my bowels! Oh, my navel! Oh, my whole body,
poor wretch!" And he says: "Oh, my gout! Oh, my
lumbago! Oh, my back! Oh, my kidneys! Oh, my

rheumatism! Oh, my bellyache! Oh, my toothache!"
So he groans and she scolds, and day and night they
quarrel and curse their servants. They are discon-
tented with themselves and nothing pleases them;
scowling, red in the face, sad and forlorn. They
abhor all festivities and are tormented by pleasures.
They are rotten in their flesh, flabby, filthy, and
spitting. Their money and wealth are of little good
to them; nor is anything in the world a help to them
in their old age, or to their pains and travails, or
to their dying or merely staying alive. So you see
what an accursed marriage this is, what pleasure,
what love, what suffering, what a blessing, what a
good fortune! May your marriage do you a lot of
good, old man, since you are so happy in it, and the
same to you, good mother! Go live with your affliction! The worst of it is, that they have no children,
nor can they have any, or even a hope of them, and
so they live out their miserable existence.

The fourth kind of marriage is to be approved:
a youth with a maiden, a maiden with a youth. This
one is to be praised and the others avoided. In it
there must be three things: betrothal, affirmation,
and accomplishment in carnal intercourse. This you
will find described at length in the *Compendium*,
Book Six, Title Fourteen, *Of Matrimony*, in which
that marriage is blessed to which God gave love and
which the parties sought, although this love, like
any other, or even the best, is madness and vanity,
for only the love of God gives life, health, wealth,
estate, honor, and final glory to him who serves
Him and cares not for vanity or madness.

I shall refrain from pursuing further the said hu-

mors, lest I be long-winded, for he who is inclined
to good works will understand well enough what
I have said, and especially since those who are influ-
enced by the four humors are as I described them,
or even so much worse that they defy description.
But, as I have said, each body contains within itself
all the four humors and complexions together, and
if the bad ones predominate over the good, they
make greatly for evil, and vice versa, for each is
modified by the others. On the other hand, feeling,
good sense, and judgment aid men and women in
no small degree to conceal a predominant bad quality, so that he who has sense, if he feels that he is
proud, will avoid as much as possible having words
with another, and will turn his back before his rage
overcomes him. And he who corrects his vices in
time, and who recognizes them before they become
malignant, does no little thing. He is master of himself, just as he who does the contrary is his own
enemy, for he carries his enemies with him and does
not provide himself with arms to protect himself
from them.

Oh, how many enemies has wretched man! Who
are they? I will tell you: the world, the devil, and
woman, woman above all! And then these evil
humors and their perverse aberrations, making him
persist in his evil ways to the end. Many are the
snares spread in this wicked world to catch the
wretched soul that does not protect itself. It has
still other enemies: its disordered willfulness, unbridled cupidity, intemperate anger, and premedi-
tated vengeance. Let him who desires eternal life
open his eyes, therefore, and not move hastily or turn
his eyes at the sound of the tambourine. Let him love

God with fear. Let him fear His justice and beware of offending Him, or, if he offends Him, let him beg for mercy at once. Let him, moreover, take as his advocate the Blessed Virgin Mary, and let his heart never depart from her. Let him always commend himself to her and pray the saints of Paradise incessantly to guard him, help him, and defend him, lest at the moment of his death he be caught in mortal sin. Let him die knowing God, that he may repent of the sins he has committed, and God, who is all-powerful, will protect him and give him His grace and blessing. And may He permit us to love Him and serve Him in such wise that we shall deserve to achieve His glory, amen!

Here ends the third part of this book and work.

↰ Notes

1. "Juan de Ausim," also described as "a Doctor of Paris," has not been identified. Mario Penna, the latest (1955) editor of the book, has established that the Archpriest owes a very large number of passages to the *De amore* of Andrea Capellanus, who may, therefore, be the original of "Juan de Ausim."

2. *Cañas* was a game in which mounted teams dashed at each other armed with canes and shields; a mock jousting.

3. *Borrincos,* to judge by the context, were a kind of spring fruit.

4. "Imprimas" is associated with Epicurus in the passage: "Asy les contesce como fizo a los dos sabios, Epicurio e Ynprimas, que nunca su dyos de Epicurio era synon comer, e de Ynprimas sinon beber." Professor H. R. W. Smith makes the teasing suggestion that perhaps "Imprimas" may have arisen through a misreading of Lucretius, where *primum* and *primus* occur in a number of places in the *De rerum natura,* and may have been mistaken for proper names. It may be, on the other hand, that the Archpriest needed a drinking *sabio* to balance Epicurus, who in mediaeval folklore was a glutton.

5. "Trotaconventos" first appears in *El libro de buen amor* of Juan Ruiz, Archpriest of Hita, in the fourteenth century. She is a go-between, messenger, procuress, midwife, and witch, and finally emerges as the Celestina in 1499.

198

6. *Lençareja* or *lencereja*, to judge by the context, was a simple garment or headdress, probably of linen (*lienzo*). I have rendered it by "linen kerchief."

7. *Angelores* was evidently an ingredient of a preparation for whitening the skin.

8. "Collares de oro e *de medio partido*," that is, gold necklaces of some kind.

9. *Anosegados* and *manbre* occur in the passage: "los dientes anosegados o fregados con manbre, yerva que llaman de Yndia."

10. "Scotland" and the city of "Salustria" occur in the passage: "Uno onbre muy sabio era en las partes de levante, en el rregno de Escocia, en una cibdad por nonbre Salustria." The Archpriest's geography may be a bit weak, but it is a pleasant thought.

11. "Sidrach" occurs in the passage: "E en tal manera nos avemos que de aquel verdadero Sydrach, Jesuchristo, . . . seamos amados." This figure had me baffled until Professor E. B. Place ran down Sidrach for me. Sidrach, it seems, was a thirteenth-century Jewish or Arabic encyclopedist who evidently enjoyed a reputation for immense learning. An early (Paris, 1528) edition of his book is entitled *Sidrach le grant philosophe: Fontaine de toutes les sciences*. Jesus, who was omniscient, thus becomes the "true" Sidrach, naturally enough!

12. *Canusos* occurs in the passage: "rromos, canusos, o grandes narizes e luengas." In the context it ought to apply to noses, but *canusos* or *canosos* means "whitehaired."

Bibliography

(Note: I am listing here only the studies and editions of *The Archpriest of Talavera* that I have consulted in my translation. The interested reader will find a more detailed bibliography in Mario Penna's edition, q.v. below.)

MENÉNDEZ Y PELAYO, MARCELINO, *Orígenes de la novela*, Vol. I, pp. cx–cxx. (Madrid, 1905.)

PENNA, MARIO, *Arcipreste de Talavera*, edito da M. P. Paleographic and critical edition. (Torino, 1955.)

PÉREZ PASTOR, CRISTÓBAL, *El Arcipreste de Talavera*, por el bachiller Alfonso Martínez de Toledo. Paleographic edition. (Madrid, 1901.)

SIMPSON, LESLEY BYRD, *El Arcipreste de Talavera*. Paleographic edition. (Berkeley, 1939.)

STEIGER, ARNOLD, "Contribución al estudio del vocabulario del Corbacho," *Boletín de la Real Academia Española*, 1922–1923.